MATCHSTICK MODELLING

MATCHSTICK MODELLING

Roy Ashley

Photographs by Peter Hirst-Smith

PELHAM BOOKS

*To my wife, without whose
patience and perseverance this book
would never have been written.*

First published in Great Britain by
Pelham Books Ltd
44 & 45 Bedford Square
London WC1B 3EF
1979

ISBN 0 7207 1150 9

Photoset by Northampton Phototypesetters Ltd and
printed and bound in Great Britain by
Hazell Watson and Viney Ltd, Aylesbury, Bucks

CONTENTS

Windmill, see p. 45

INTRODUCTION

Over the past ten years or so, matchstick – or splint – modelling has become a very popular hobby, and this book is designed not only to give instruction to beginners, but also to offer a challenge to more advanced matchstick-modellers. It explains the different methods of modelling that can be used and gives step-by-step instructions for making a variety of models, from a simple wishing well, using only 750 matches, to a gypsy caravan which, when decorated, would need over 10,000.

Ways of decorating the models are suggested, but there is plenty of scope for the modeller to use his imagination and adapt the decorations, and the models themselves, to produce entirely original designs.

TOOLS, MATERIALS AND METHODS

You will need only a few basic tools and materials and most are easily available from an ordinary hardware or do-it-yourself shop, or from an artists' supply shop. Those listed below are what you will need to make most of the models in this book. Any extra tools or materials are specified at the beginning of each chapter.

TOOLS

Cutting board – an ordinary bread board, approx. 38 × 30cm (15 × 12in) would be fine.

Knife – with a long pointed cutting blade and a firm grip for basic modelling. A Stanley knife is ideal.

 – for intricate carving you will need a finer bladed knife, such as a Stanley modelling knife or a surgeon's scalpel.

Geometry set – (available from Woolworths) or a set of compasses, small set square, protractor

30cm (12in) rule

Sanding block

Sandpaper – a selection of grades from coarse (A2 40) to very fine (A2 180, A2 220)

Carpenters' snips (pincers)

Ordinary scissors

Small fine file

MATERIALS

Matches/splints – contact Bryant and May Ltd, Match Manufacturers, Fairfield Rd, London E3, who can supply direct or give the address of your nearest stockist.

Glue – any whitewood glue; Evo-Stik Woodworking Adhesive is good, and easily applied from the fine nozzle of the tube. It can be wiped off any surface with a damp cloth, but *do not* wipe a model because this will unstick the matches. Always use sandpaper to remove excess glue.

Cardboard – 2 grades of cardboard are used: thick (approx. 225 grams) or thin (approx. 160 grams). These are specified for each model.

Perspex – 2 thicknesses: 1mm (thick) and 0.5mm (thin); these also are specified where used.

Varnish – clear polyurethane

13mm ($\frac{1}{2}$in) brush for varnishing

Dressmakers' pins

Strong elastic bands

Tubes of acrylic paint (such as Reeves) in primary colours

Accessories: musical works for the cigarette box or clock works for the grandfather clock can be obtained from modelling shops. W. Hobby Ltd, Knight's Hill Square, London SE27 OHH, have a very wide range of accessories and an extensive catalogue which can be obtained through the post.

METHOD I

Method 1 is most appropriate for making simple models such as the wine and table mats or the wishing well. For ease of reference, the instructions given for making the models in this book all follow Method 1, but the models could equally well be made using Methods 2 and 3.

Cut out the templates (patterns) needed for the model in cardboard.

Apply a generous coat of glue along the length of the template, but only to a depth of

Fig.1

6mm ($\frac{1}{4}$in)

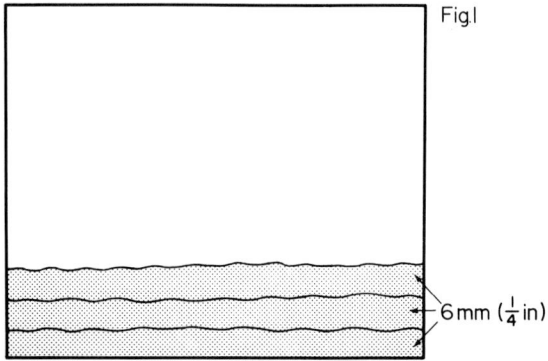

6mm ($\frac{1}{4}$in) in from the edge (see Fig. 1). This allows plenty of time for placing the first matches in position before the glue begins to set. Do not cover the whole of the template with glue all at once or it will dry before you have time to stick on all the matches. There is no need to put glue on each individual match, except when you are decorating a finished model.

Start matching one side of the template in 6mm ($\frac{1}{4}$in) stages, making sure that the matches interlock (Fig. 2). Otherwise when you are assembling the model it will tend to twist out of shape.

Make sure that as you press each match onto the glue, you pull it towards the match already laid, so that the glue sticks one match to the next as well as holding them to the template.

When one side is completely matched, trim the edges with pincers or a Stanley modelling knife.

Always allow templates to dry for 2 hours at least, unless otherwise specified. While drying, the model must be pressed against a flat surface

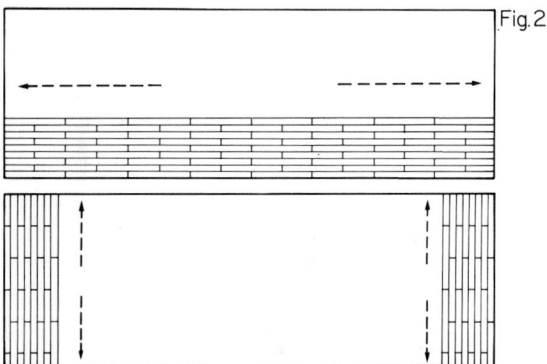

to prevent warping. One way of doing this is to use a press.

To make a press you will need:

2 pieces hardboard or 6mm ($\frac{1}{4}$in) plywood, 45cm (18in) square
4 6mm ($\frac{1}{4}$in) wing nuts and bolts
6mm ($\frac{1}{4}$in) drill

Drill a hole in each corner of each square. Place template(s) between the squares and tighten up the nuts to apply a firm pressure to the templates (see Fig. 3). This press will take several layers of templates, one on top of the next.

When the first side is dry, match the other side, again in 6mm ($\frac{1}{4}$in) stages, making sure that the matches run in the opposite direction (see Fig. 2). This gives the model extra strength. The matches must again be interlocking and stuck to each other as well as to the template.

When this side is complete, replace in the press and allow to dry for 2 hours.

When the matched parts are dry, sand lightly, first with coarse sandpaper then with fine (see Materials p. 9). This is to level the matches so that there are no indentations and no surplus glue on the surface. Glue will be clearly visible through the varnish, so it is most important to remove every trace. Clean and square off edges with sandpaper also.

When the parts are well sanded, follow the directions given for the particular model you are making. If some parts are not needed immediately, keep them in the press to avoid warping until they are needed.

When the model is complete, finish off with 3 coats of varnish unless otherwise specified. Rub down lightly with sandpaper between each coat and allow twenty-four hours to dry between coats.

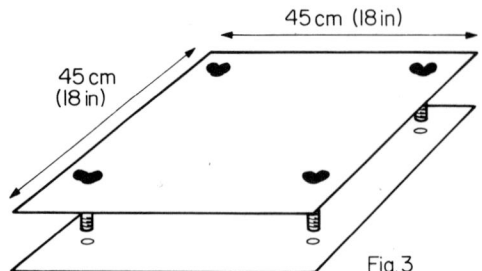

Fig. 2

45 cm (18in)

45 cm (18 in)

Fig. 3

If you wish to paint the model, apply one coat of varnish before painting. Matches are porous and if paint is applied before varnish the paint will simply run all over the model. After painting, give a final 2 coats of varnish.

Carved matches

If you use a cardboard template, it may be visible at the edges between the 2 layers of matches, depending on the construction of the model. To cover this, use carved matches.

Choose some good matches (those which are really straight and square) and notch along each edge of one side with a sharp knife as shown in Fig. 4. Stick them into place, leave to dry and then rub lightly with fine sandpaper.

For an alternative method of carving matches, see p. 38.

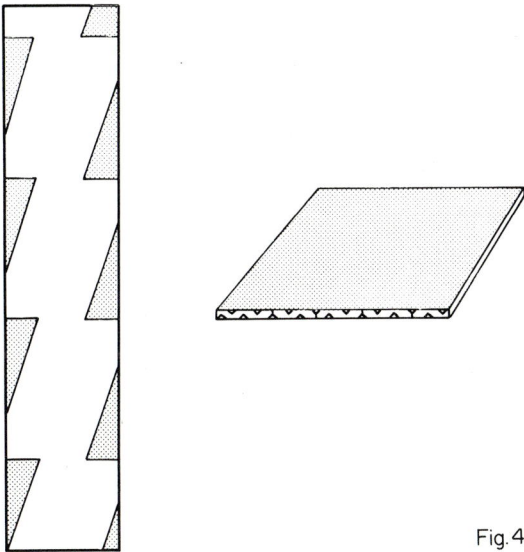

Fig. 4

METHOD 2

Method 2 is exactly the same as Method 1 except that the templates are cut out in fine tracing paper, instead of cardboard. This produces a more stable model. The use of tracing paper also means that there is no need to put a line of carved matches along any exposed edges as the tracing-paper template is not visible, while the cardboard template can be seen between the layers of matches.

METHOD 3

This is the most difficult but also the most satisfying method as it produces a model made completely of matches with no backing at all.

Cut out the templates needed for the model in flexible perspex.

Apply a generous coat of glue along the length of the template, but only to a depth of 6mm ($\frac{1}{4}$in) in from the edge (see Fig. 1).

Start matching one side of the template in 6mm ($\frac{1}{4}$in) stages, making sure that the matches interlock (Fig. 2).

Make sure that as you press each match onto the glue, you pull it towards the match already laid, so that the glue sticks one match to the next as well as holding them to the template.

When one side is completely matched, trim the edges and place in a press (see Method 1), and allow to dry for 2 hours at least.

When each part of the model is completely matched on one side and dry, remove from press and flex the perspex as in Fig. 5 to release the template.

Then place a second layer of matches again in 6mm ($\frac{1}{4}$in) stages onto each part of the model. Make sure that this second layer runs in the opposite direction to the first and that the matches are interlocking.

When the second layer is complete, trim, allow to dry for 2 hours in the press and sand down as Method 1. Then assemble the model according to the instructions.

The two important things to remember for all three methods are:

1) that the matches must always be interlocking
2) that the matches on one side of the template must run in the opposite direction to those on the other side.

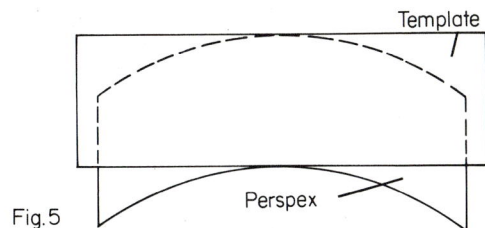

Fig. 5

Template

Perspex

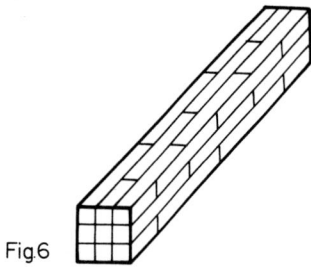
Fig.6

Most models also need parts which are made of solid blocks of matches, with no template. It is important to interlock these blocks both widthways, lengthways and depthways, (Fig. 6) otherwise they will simply fall apart.

Measuring
The instructions are given in both Imperial and Metric measures. Do not compare the measurements, as the conversions are not always accurate, they may even differ: $\frac{1}{2}$in might be interpreted as 10mm here and 15mm there. This is because the metric equivalent given is always the nearest *practical* measurement which is most suitable in each specific instance, ensuring that the finished model is in proportion.

Guitar, see p. 30

TABLE MATS AND MATCHING WINE MATS

Table mats and wine mats are very easy to make and therefore ideal for the beginner.

The instructions given here follow Method 1 and matching both sides, but the mats may be matched on one side only if you prefer, and made according to any of the three methods.

You will need:

1500 matches
Cardboard (225 grams) for templates:
  6 25cm (10in) × 18cm (7in)
  6 8cm (3in) × 8cm (3in)

First cut out templates as above, using a set square to ensure that corners are square to a right angle.

To make the simple pattern shown in Fig. 7, use a pencil and mark the templates lightly as shown in Figs. 8 and 9 (overleaf).

Apply glue along the length of the face side of the template to a width of 6mm ($\frac{1}{4}$in) in from the edge. Following the pattern traced on the template, lay matches in 6mm ($\frac{1}{4}$in) stages, (Method 1), working from the outside towards the centre. Remember to interlock matches (Fig. 2) on this outer strip and stick them to each other as well as to the template.

At each corner, cut matches to diagonal line.

When you have completed the outer strip of the pattern, lay a line of matches either side

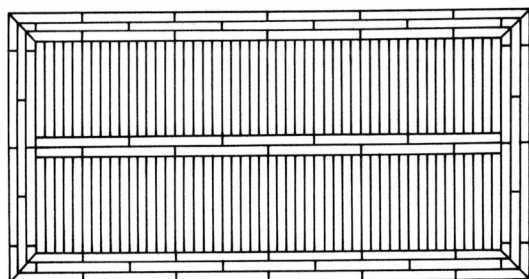

Face side

Reverse side

Fig. 7

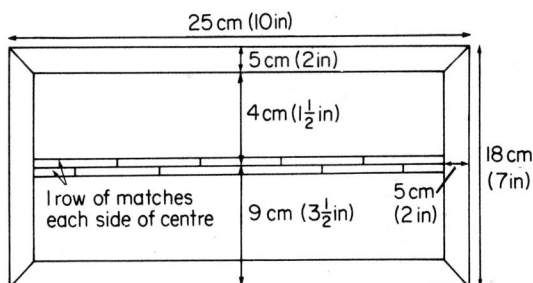

25 cm (10in)

5 cm (2 in)

4 cm (1½ in)

18 cm (7 in)

1 row of matches each side of centre

9 cm (3½ in)

5 cm (2 in)

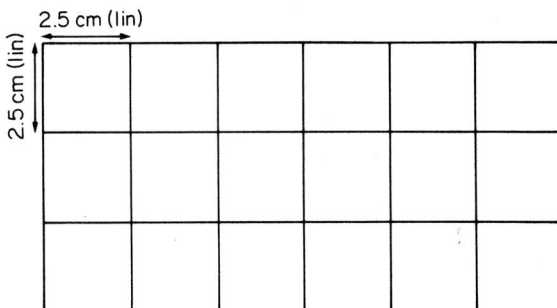

2.5 cm (1in)

2.5 cm (1in)

Fig. 8

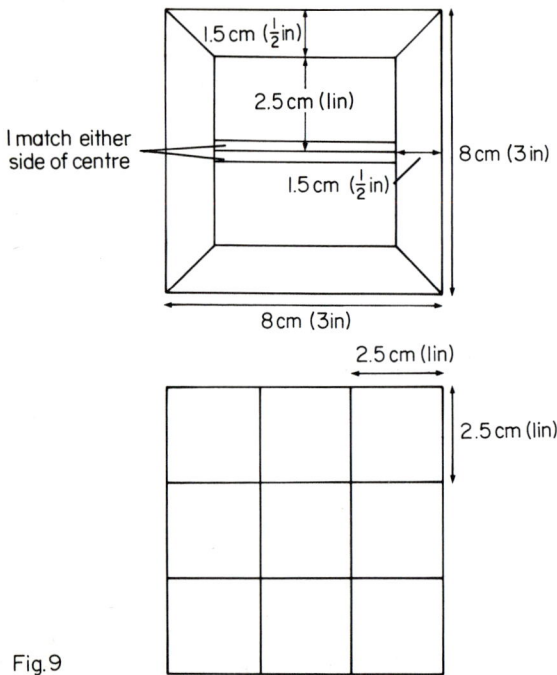

Fig. 9

ready to match it on the reverse side, otherwise it may warp.

As the first side of each mat dries, remove from the press, glue and match the reverse side. Start at one edge and match straight across to the other, again only laying the glue in stages to avoid it drying out before you have laid all the matches.

Trim, place in the press and allow to dry.

Take one mat at a time from the press and use a sanding block and coarse sandpaper to clean off surplus glue from both sides, cleaning and squaring up the four edges. Sand both sides until they are completely level, with no indentations.

Then use fine sandpaper to smooth off mats ready for coating with varnish.

The template will still show at the edges of the mats between the two layers of matches. To cover this, decorate with carved matches (pp. 11 or 38).

If the mats are to be left plain, finish them off with 6 coats of varnish. (The extra ·3 coats are recommended as protection against wear and tear.).Rub down lightly between coats and allow 24 hours for each to dry.

If the mats are to be decorated, for example painted with a flower design as in Fig. 10, apply one coat of varnish before painting. Otherwise the paint will simply run all over the model. Allow paint to dry for 24 hours and then apply the remaining 5 coats of varnish.

of the centre line, then fill in the remaining sides, cutting the matches to size.

As each template is matched on one side, trim the edges with pincers or Stanley modelling knife. Put in the press and leave to dry for two hours. You are unlikely to match all the mats in one session, but if you do the press can hold them all, in layers on top of each other.

Leave each mat in the press until you are

Fig. 10

WISHING WELL

You will need:

Approx. 750 matches
Templates: 225 gram cardboard
   1 piece 13cm (5in) × 13cm (5in) base
   1 piece 13cm (5in) × 10cm (4in) roof
Templates: 160 gram cardboard
   1 piece 30cm (12in) × 4.5cm (1¾in) outer wall
   1 piece 25cm (10in) × 4.5cm (1¾in) inner wall
Bradawl
Short length of fine chain or thread
Large thimble or similar-shaped object for bucket mould

Make according to Method 1, unless otherwise specified.

Cut out templates as above.

Match the base in 6mm (¼in) stages as Method 1, one side at a time, interlocking the matches and making sure that they run in opposite directions on either side. As each side is matched, place in the press until dry.

Mark out roof as in Fig. 11, leaving a gap for the fold, and match each side as in Fig. 12.

When the base and roof are completely matched, leave in the press until needed again.

Match the inner and outer walls widthways, one side at a time, and in the same direction on *both* sides, otherwise they will not bend to form a circle. *Do not* place them in the press, for the same reason. Just put on one side and they will tend to curl round of their own accord.

For the 2 uprights which support the roof and for the rotating pin which carries the bucket, make up 3 solid lengths 15cm (6in) long, 4 matches wide and 4 matches deep. Interlock each layer as you do it. Shape one

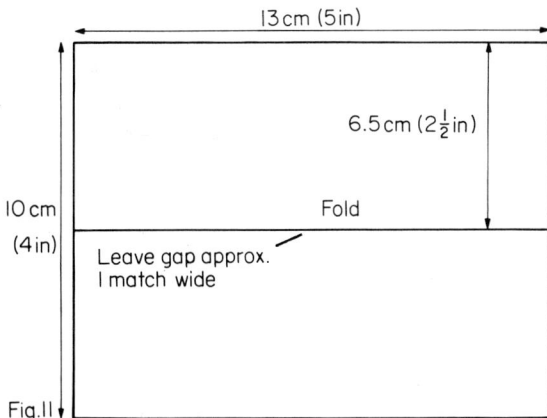

13cm (5in)

6.5cm (2½in)

10 cm
(4in)

Fold

Leave gap approx.
1 match wide

Fig. 11

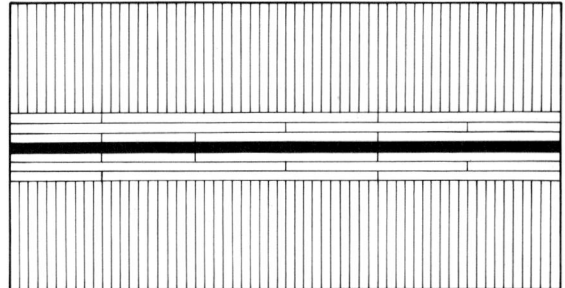

Face side

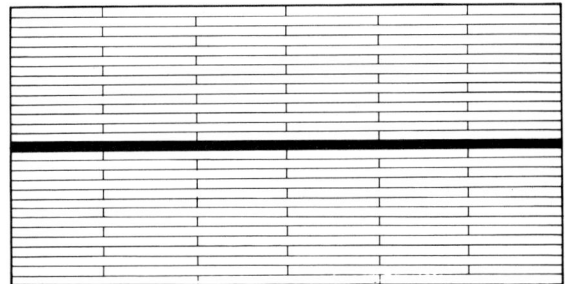

Reverse side

Fig. 12

15

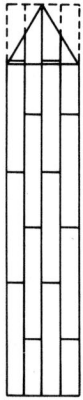

Fig. 13

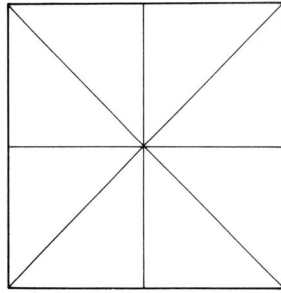

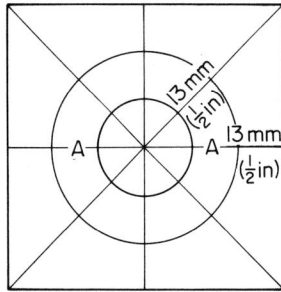

Fig. 14

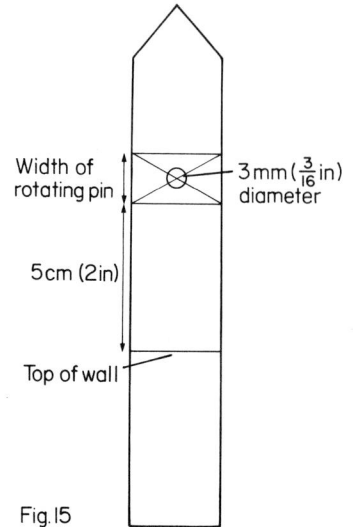

Fig. 15

end of each as shown in Fig. 13.

When they are dry, rub down all parts with coarse and then fine sandpaper, removing all traces of glue and indentations.

Mark out the base, in stages as shown in Fig. 14. The edge of the outer circle should be 13mm ($\frac{1}{2}$in) in from the edge of the base; the edge of the inner circle 13mm ($\frac{1}{2}$in) in from the outer circle, as shown. Trim off surplus round the outer circle.

The uprights are fixed at points A. Make sure that the bottoms of the uprights are perfectly flat and square. Then apply glue to them one at a time and stick to the base. Use a small set square to ensure that they are upright.

Allow to dry overnight before attempting to fix the well walls.

To fix the walls: trim one end of the inner wall so that it is perfectly straight. Apply glue to the inside of the uprights, from the base to the height of the wall (4.5cm (1$\frac{3}{4}$in)), and along the bottom of the inner wall.

Glue the inner wall so that the trimmed edge comes half way across the inside of one upright and then follow round the inner circle on the base, pressing the wall onto the base and against the inside of the upright on the other side, until the two ends meet. Trim off any

excess with a Stanley modelling knife. Hold the wall against the uprights until the glue takes.

Repeat this procedure for the outer wall, fixing to the outside of the uprights. Allow 2 or 3 hours to dry completely.

To fill in the hollow between the inner and outer walls, cut approximately 100 matches in half. Lay glue in stages of about 13mm ($\frac{1}{2}$in) at a time along both walls and lay the matches across them. Allow to dry, trim off any overhang and sand to a smooth finish.

Rotating pin

Mark the uprights as shown in Fig. 15. Use the bradawl to make the holes. Then hold the rotating pin across the uprights, flush at one end and overrunning at the other by approximately 13mm ($\frac{1}{2}$in) for the handle, as shown in Fig. 16.

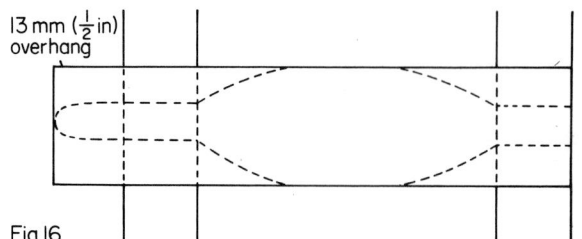

Fig. 16

Plate 1: Wishing well

Mark the rotating pin as shown and then use the Stanley knife and sandpaper to shape.

Using thumb and forefinger, pull the 2 uprights slightly apart and fit the 2 pegs into the holes.

Roof

Apply glue to the pointed tops of the uprights. Fix roof over them and apply pressure until the glue sets.

Use the bradawl to make a hole through the centre of the rotating pin. Thread one end of the chain through it and secure.

Bucket

Make up a small square of matches, 1 match thick and 2.5cm (1in) square. Place the bottom of the thimble onto the centre of this square.

Using the thimble as a mould, match round it, making sure that the matches are glued to the base as well as to each other.

Before the matches dry, remove the thimble and trim round the base. This will give you the shape of the bucket. When it is dry, trim to the size required, sand and varnish.

To make handles, glue part matches into a curve, allow to dry and then sand down and glue to sides. Varnish. Fix bucket securely to the other end of the chain or thread.

Now the model is complete, take a worn piece of fine sandpaper and lightly go over each part again.

Then apply 3 coats of varnish, rubbing down lightly between each coat and allowing 24 hours between coats to dry.

Plate 2: Wishing well – detail of bucket and handle

NORMAN CHURCH

Before cutting out the templates, decide whether the model is to be matched on one side only or on both. When assembled the church will form a hollow shell before being mounted on the base, so if you match it on one side only the cardboard used for the template will need to be thicker than if both sides are matched.

You will need:

Matches – 1000 for matching one side, 2000 for matching both
Cardboard – either 225 grams (thick) or 160 grams (thin) for templates:
   2 18cm (7in) × 33cm (13in) sides
   1 20.5cm (8in) × 25cm (10in) steeple
   1 38cm (15in) × 25cm (10in) tower
   1 23cm (9in) × 13cm (5in) for exact fitting base; before cutting out see *base* p. 22
Perspex – 1 sheet 15cm (6in) square
Dressmakers' pins
Coloured paper
30.5cm (12in) ruler
Needle

Cut out, very precisely, templates A–E (Figs 17 and 18), using compasses to get the basic shape of the steeple. Mark the dotted 'fold' lines on both sides of the templates. Use a set square to ensure that corners form true right angles. If the templates are not cut out very accurately, when the parts are assembled the model will be out of square and useless. Cut out windows and doors as marked and put them all to one side except for one of the doors which can be discarded.

The roof, tower, steeple and sides should be matched as indicated in Figs 17 and 18.

Apply glue along one side of the templates,

Plate 3: Norman church – rear view

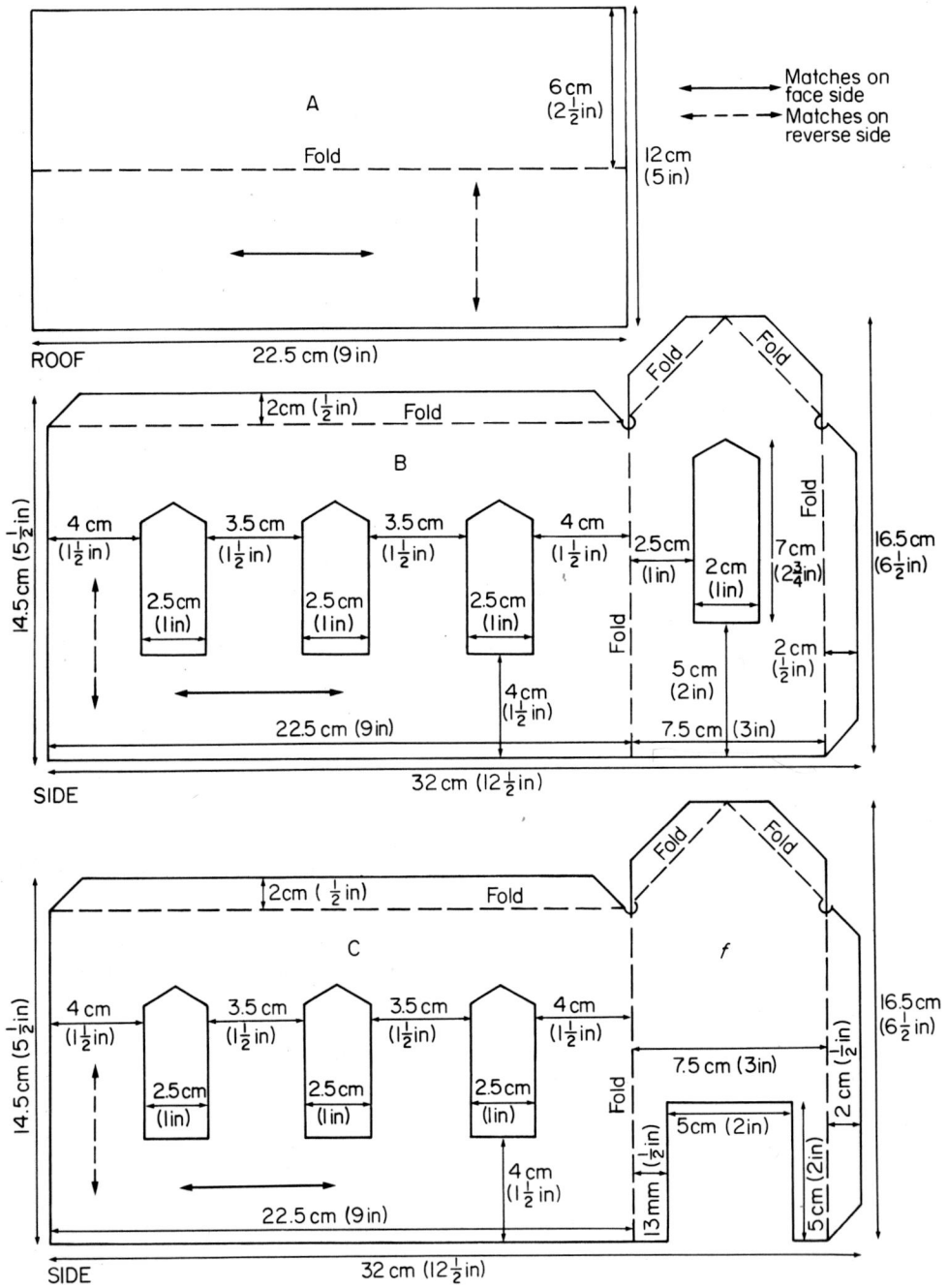

A

Fold

6 cm
(2½in)

12 cm
(5 in)

←——→ Matches on
face side
←— — —→ Matches on
reverse side

ROOF   22.5 cm (9 in)

2cm (½in)   Fold

Fold   Fold

B

Fold

14.5 cm (5½in)

4 cm
(1½in)

3.5 cm
(1½in)

3.5 cm
(1½in)

4 cm
(1½in)

2.5cm
(1in)

2.5cm
(1in)

2.5cm
(1in)

2.5cm
(1in)

2cm
(1in)

7cm
(2¾in)

Fold

16.5 cm
(6½in)

2 cm
(½in)

5 cm
(2in)

Fold

4 cm
(1½in)

22.5 cm (9 in)

7.5 cm (3in)

SIDE   32 cm (12½in)

2cm (½in)   Fold

Fold   Fold

C

Fold

f

14.5 cm (5½in)

4 cm
(1½in)

3.5 cm
(1½in)

3.5 cm
(1½in)

4 cm
(1½in)

2.5cm
(1in)

2.5cm
(1in)

2.5cm
(1in)

7.5 cm (3in)

2 cm (½in)

16.5 cm
(6½in)

Fold

5cm (2in)

5 cm (2in)

3mm (½in)

4 cm
(1½in)

22.5 cm (9 in)

SIDE   32 cm (12½in)

Fig.17

20

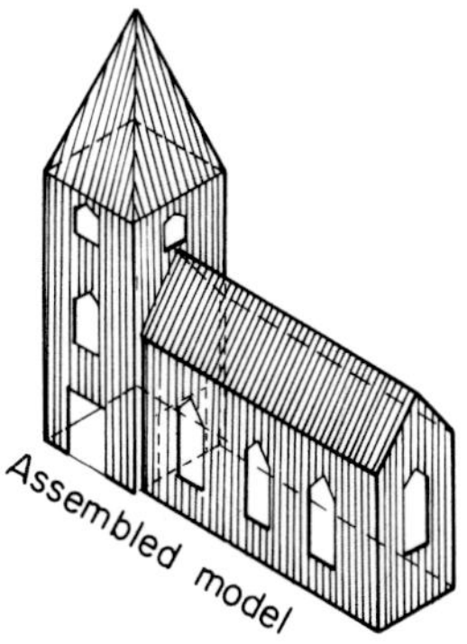

Assembled model

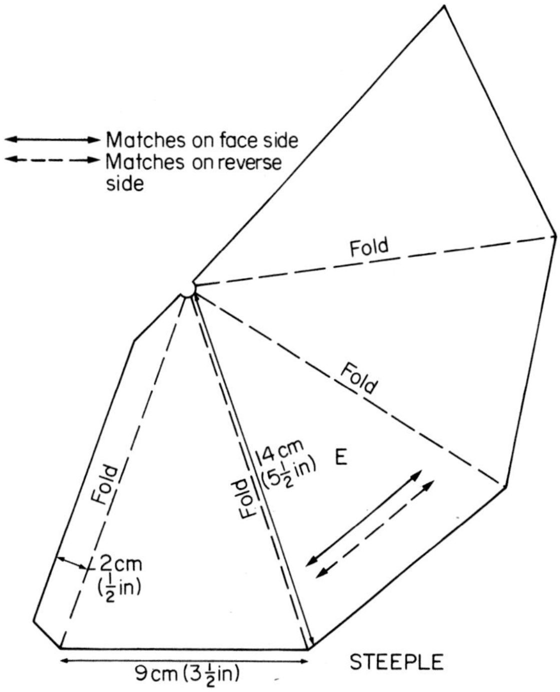

Matches on face side
Matches on reverse side

Fold

Fold

Fold

Fold

14 cm (5½ in) E

2 cm (½ in)

9 cm (3½ in) STEEPLE

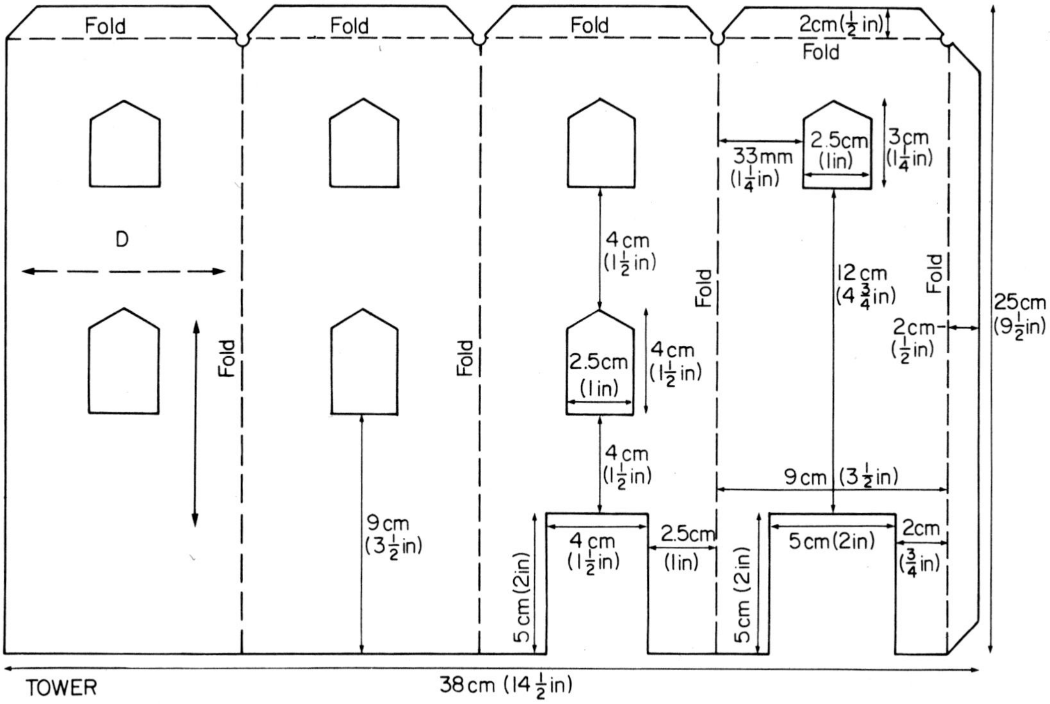

Fold   Fold   Fold   2cm(½ in)
                        Fold

D

Fold   Fold   Fold

2.5cm
(1in)   3cm
         (1¼in)

33mm
(1¼in)

4 cm
(1½ in)

4 cm
(1½ in)

2.5cm
(1in)   4 cm
         (1½ in)

12 cm
(4¾ in)

2cm
(½in)

9cm (3½ in)

4 cm
(1½ in)

9cm
(3½in)

5 cm (2in)   4 cm
              (1½ in)   2.5cm
                         (1in)   5 cm (2in)   2cm
                                                (¾in)

5cm (2 in)

25cm
(9½in)

TOWER   38 cm (14½ in)

Fig.18

to a depth of 6mm ($\frac{1}{4}$in) and lay matches in 6mm ($\frac{1}{4}$in) stages across the template.

Do not match over the joining tabs or the lines marked 'fold' (leave approximately 1 match width free), and cut the matches to size at the end of each row. Do not leave this until each template is completely matched – you may find it difficult to trim off all the ends at once and consequently cut through joining tabs.

Remember that matches must interlock (Fig. 2) and stick to each other as well as to the template.

Do not fold any part until the model has been completely matched and is ready for assembly.

As each template is completely matched on one side, place it in the press (p. 10) and allow to dry for 2 hours at least.

When they are dry, remove the templates one at a time and match on the reverse side. Remember that these matches must run in the opposite direction to those on the front. The steeple is an exception to this and can be matched in the same way on both sides.

When completely matched each part should be put back in the press to dry and kept there until required again, to prevent warping.

Take one part at a time from the press and use a sanding block and coarse sandpaper to clean off surplus glue from both sides, cleaning and squaring up the edges. Sand both sides until they are completely level, with no indentations. Then use fine sandpaper to smooth off ready for varnishing.

Assembly

The model is now ready to assemble. Fold carefully along the lines marked 'fold' on each template. Put glue on joining tabs and fix these to the inside of the adjoining parts, pressing together with your fingers until they have taken hold. In this way join the roof to the sides; the tower to the steeple.

Allow these to dry for about 2 hours. Then glue the door end of the main body of the church (*f*) and stick firmly to the side marked *f* of the tower, so that the two door openings meet, again pressing together with your fingers until the glue holds.

Carved match frame

Fig.19

Windows

Place window templates cut out earlier on a sheet of thin perspex. Draw round the edges in pencil and cut out.

For *clear windows* use a ruler and fine needle to mark as shown in Fig. 19 (left), starting with a diagonal line from corner to corner.

For *stained glass windows* criss-cross the perspex with a needle as above, and then glue pieces of coloured paper to the back, to make a pattern such as that in Fig. 19 (right).

The window frames are made using carved matches (p. 11). Sand down lightly with fine sandpaper. Stick a line of carved matches (1 wide) round each window. Allow to dry and then glue frames round the edges of window spaces on sides and tower.

Base

The base can either be cut to fit the bottom of the church exactly, or it may be larger to hold scenery such as trees or a picket fence, so you must first decide how large you would like it to be. Details for making a fence are given below.

If the base is to fit the church exactly, place the model onto a piece of cardboard, draw round the outside in pencil and cut out. Match on both sides as for other parts above and in Method 1 (p. 9), remembering to interlock the matches and to have them going in opposite directions on either side.

Sand down to remove excess glue and any indentations, first with a coarse sandpaper and then with fine.

When dry, glue to bottom of church.

Doors
Take 2 door templates and mark the pattern in Fig. 20 lightly in pencil on both sides. Following pattern, match one side at a time. First match along diagonals, then fill in the sides. Allow to dry. Sand to a smooth finish.

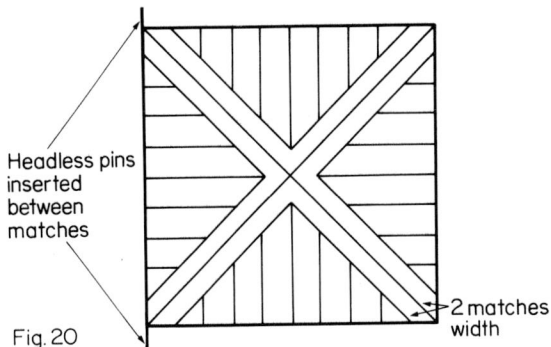

Fig. 20

Headless pins inserted between matches

2 matches width

The doors can either be glued permanently into place or hinged.

To hinge the doors, use dressmakers' pins, first removing the heads. Insert pins into the top and bottom edge of the door between layers of matches (see Fig. 20) allowing about 3mm ($\frac{1}{8}$in) to protrude. Then insert the protruding pins between the layers of matches of the door opening (see Fig. 21) at the top and into the base at the bottom. If the sides are matched on one side only, the pins will go between the matches and the cardboard template.

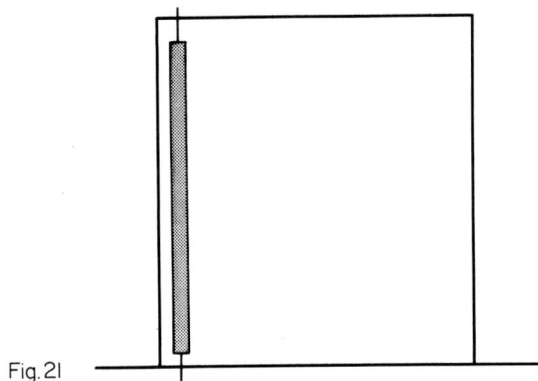

Fig. 21

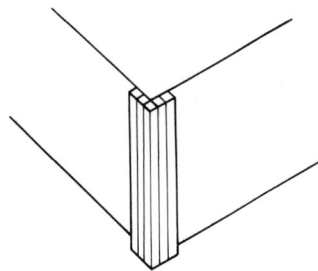

Fig. 22

To make a handle for the door, glue 2 matches together. Glue a third match on top of them, in the centre. When dry, cut in half and discard one half. Cut the other in half again and sand down lightly. Then glue one piece to each door.

Corners
At this stage each corner of the model will show the template. To cover these make up for each corner 1 strip 2 matches wide, 1 match deep, and 1 strip 3 matches wide, 1 match deep, to the required length. Allow to dry, then sand to a smooth finish.

Glue one of the wider strips to the side of one corner, overlapping the corner by 1 match width. Then glue the narrower strip to the adjoining side so that it butts up to the overlapping match (see Fig. 22). Repeat this for each corner.

An alternative way of finishing off the corner joints of the tower and steeple is shown for the grandfather clock, p. 38. For extra decoration, add carved matches to the corner joints.

When the model is complete, sand down one last time with a worn piece of fine sandpaper, so that every surface is perfectly smooth.

Then apply 3 coats of varnish, rubbing down lightly between coats and allowing 24 hours for each coat to dry.

Fencing
If you decide to make a larger base, you could put a fence round it. For the horizontal bars of the fence, make up 2 strips 2 matches

wide, the length of the base; 2 strips 2 matches wide, the width of the base.

For the uprights, use ¾ matches, and carve if you wish (p. 11). Assemble as Fig. 23, allow to dry, sand down and varnish. Then glue round the edge of the base.

The method used to construct the church can

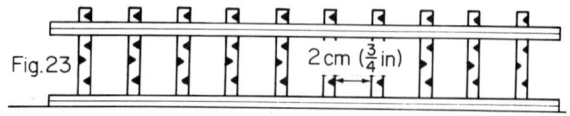

be used for all sorts of buildings – you could build an entire village with houses, pub, garage, railway station, farm, etc.

Plate 4: Norman church – detail of windows and carved matches

Plate 5: Norman church

CIGARETTE BOX

It is necessary to match both sides of the templates for this model, to give it stability.

You will need:

1250 matches
Cardboard (225 grams) for templates:
   1 15cm (6in) × 10cm (4in) base
   1 16.5cm (6½in) × 11.5cm (4½in) lid
   2 14.5cm (5¾in) × 4cm (1½in) sides
   2 9.5cm (3¾in) × 4cm (1½in) ends

Cut out templates as above very precisely, using a set square to make sure that the corners are square to a right angle. A pattern for the lid and base is shown in Fig. 24. Mark this lightly in pencil on the templates.

The sides and ends should be matched lengthways on the outside, widthways on the inside. Apply glue along the length of the template, to a depth of 6mm (¼in) in from the edge, and lay matches in 6mm (¼in) stages across the rest of the template, remembering to interlock matches (Fig. 2).

For the pattern on the face sides of the lid and base, first form the central cross, then the diagonals, then fill in round these, cutting matches to size. Remember to glue only the part you are about to match, not the whole template.

As each piece is finished, put it in the press (p. 10) and leave to dry for 2 hours. When they are dry, remove and match the reverse sides, this time matching all parts from one edge to the other, in stages. Trim and return to the press to dry. Leave there until required again, to prevent warping.

Take one part at a time from the press and use a sanding block and coarse sandpaper to clean off surplus glue from both sides, cleaning and squaring off edges. Sand both sides until they are completely level, with no indentations. Then use a fine sandpaper to smooth down ready for varnishing.

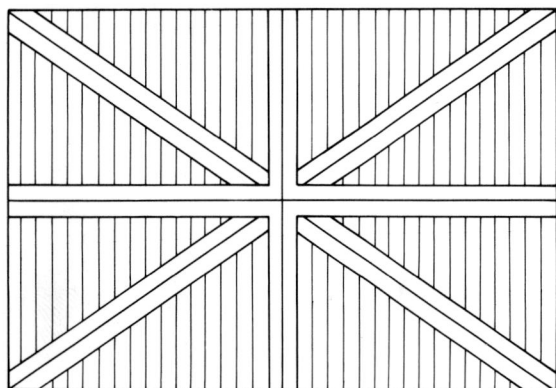

Face side

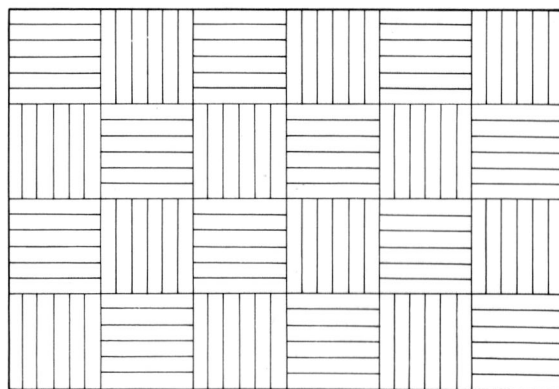

Reverse side

Fig. 24

Plate 6: Cigarette/musical jewel box

Assembly

Draw a line A just inside the edge of the base all the way round (see Fig. 25), then glue on a single row of matches round the inside of the pencil mark to form a frame. Allow to dry for 30 minutes.

Apply a small quantity of glue to the bottom of the sides and ends and fix to the base on the outside of the 1-match frame (Fig. 26). Allow 30 minutes to dry.

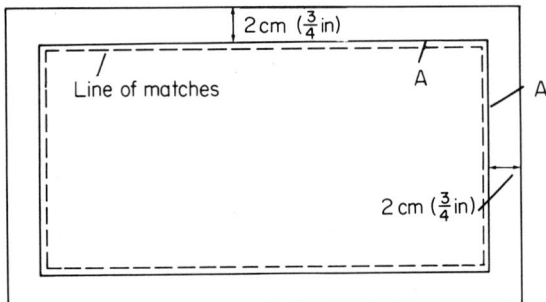

Fig.25

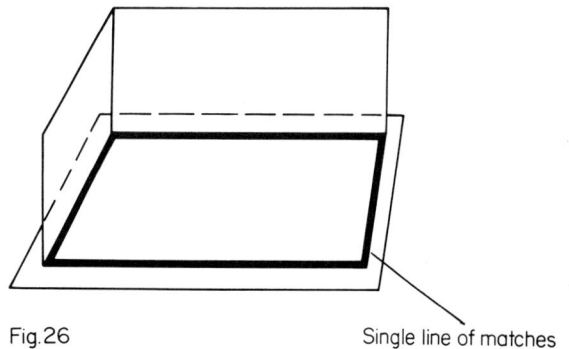

Fig.26

Single line of matches

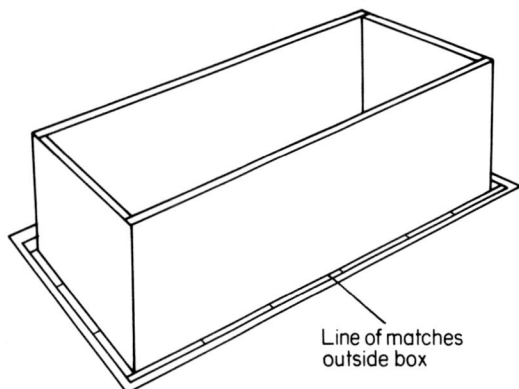

Fig. 27

Line of matches
outside box

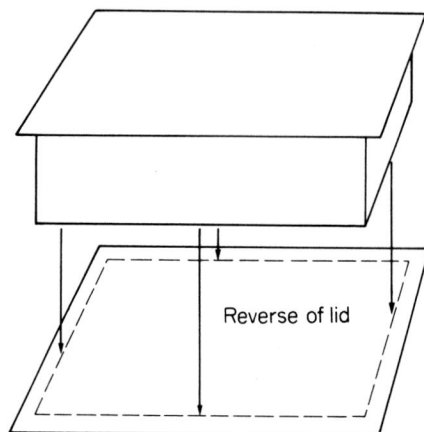

Fig. 28

Reverse of lid

Glue another line of single matches to the base along the outside of the sides and ends (see Fig. 27) and allow 30 minutes to dry. This will hold the box frame steady.

When the box is completely dry, rub off any surplus glue with fine sandpaper. Do not leave any glue on the model as it will be clearly visible through the varnish.

To fit the lid, place it upside-down on a firm surface and cover with the box (Fig. 28), making sure it is placed absolutely square. Mark lightly with a pencil round the outside of the box. Glue a single row of matches round the outside

of the pencil line and allow to dry. Rub down lightly with fine sandpaper. The lid should now fit snugly onto the box.

To make a handle, make a block 3 matches wide, 3 matches deep, 1 match long. Allow to dry, rub down to a smooth finish and glue to the centre of the lid.

Cover any template still showing with carved matches (pp. 11 or 38).

If the box is to be left plain, finish off with 3 coats of varnish. Rub down lightly between coats and allow 24 hours for each to dry.

MUSICAL JEWEL BOX

You will need:

1250 matches
Musical works – from a local model shop or from W. Hobby (see p. 9)
3mm ($\frac{1}{8}$in) drill
Cardboard (225 grams) for templates:

1 25cm (10in) × 15cm (6in) base
1 26.5cm (10½in) × 16.5cm (6½in) lid
2 24.5cm (9¾in) × 7.5cm (3in) sides
2 14cm (5½in) × 7.5cm (3in) ends

Make up the box exactly as the cigarette box.

Then take the musical works, place in one

corner of the box and press down lightly, so that the key stub which protrudes from the bottom makes a slight indentation in the base. Drill a hole on this spot.

Measure the sides of the musical works and cut out 2 cardboard templates to house it, the width of the musical works and the height of the inside of the box. Then cut 1 template 3mm ($\frac{1}{8}$in) shorter in width. Match these on both sides as Method 1. Trim, allow to dry and sand to a smooth finish. Apply glue to the base of the musical works and fix in position.

Glue along the bottom and sides of the musical works housing and fix to the sides and base of the box, around the works, so that the shorter side butts up against the longer (Fig. 29). If you are not going to line the box with velvet, cover exposed edges with carved matches (pp. 11 or 38).

If you wish to put a top on the housing, just measure the four sides, cut out and match a template and glue into position. However, the

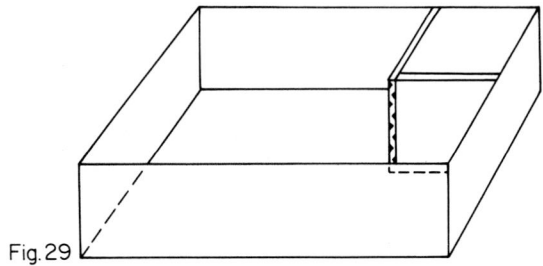

Fig. 29

musical works are quite fascinating to watch, and you may wish to leave the top open.

If you wish to line the box with velvet, first measure from the inside the base, sides, lid and musical works housing. Cut out these measurements in velvet, always allowing a little extra in the height so that the velvet will stick up above the sides and can be trimmed off neatly. Glue velvet lightly and fit round inside the box.

Finish off with 3 coats of varnish. Rub down lightly between coats and allow 24 hours for each to dry.

GUITAR

This model is particularly suitable as a wall decoration.

You will need:

Approximately 1000 matches
Templates: 225 gram cardboard:
  2 pieces 25cm (10in) × 15cm (6in) front and back (1 and 2)
  2 pieces 40cm (16in) × 5cm (2in) sides (3 and 4)
  1 piece 18cm (7in) × 4cm (1½in) top of handle (5)
  1 piece 15cm (6in) × 5cm (2in) bottom of handle (6)

Ball of string (smooth texture)
Paints or dyes

Make according to Method 1, unless otherwise specified.

Cut out templates as above. Mark out templates 1 and 2 as Fig. 30, using compasses for the curves. Match these on both sides, one side at a time. Match lengthways for 2.5cm (1in) on either side of the centre line, then match remainder as shown in Fig. 31. Remember to interlock matches. Place in press to dry. When dry, trim off surplus.

Match the reverse sides using exactly the

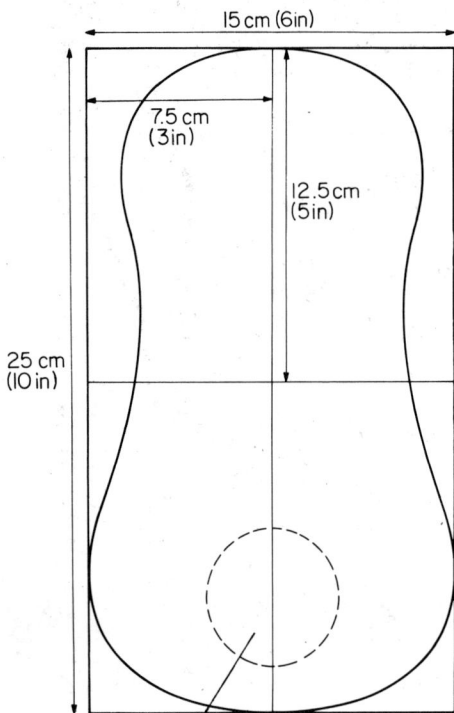

15 cm (6in)

7.5 cm (3in)

12.5 cm (5in)

25 cm (10 in)

Cut out 5.5 cm (2¼in) diameter hole in one template only

Fig. 30

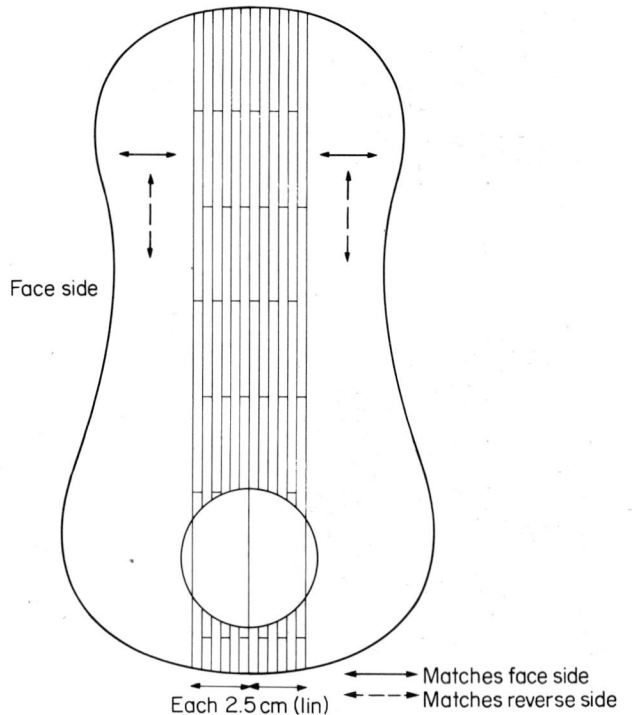

Face side

Each 2.5 cm (1in)

→ Matches face side
⤏ Matches reverse side

Fig. 31

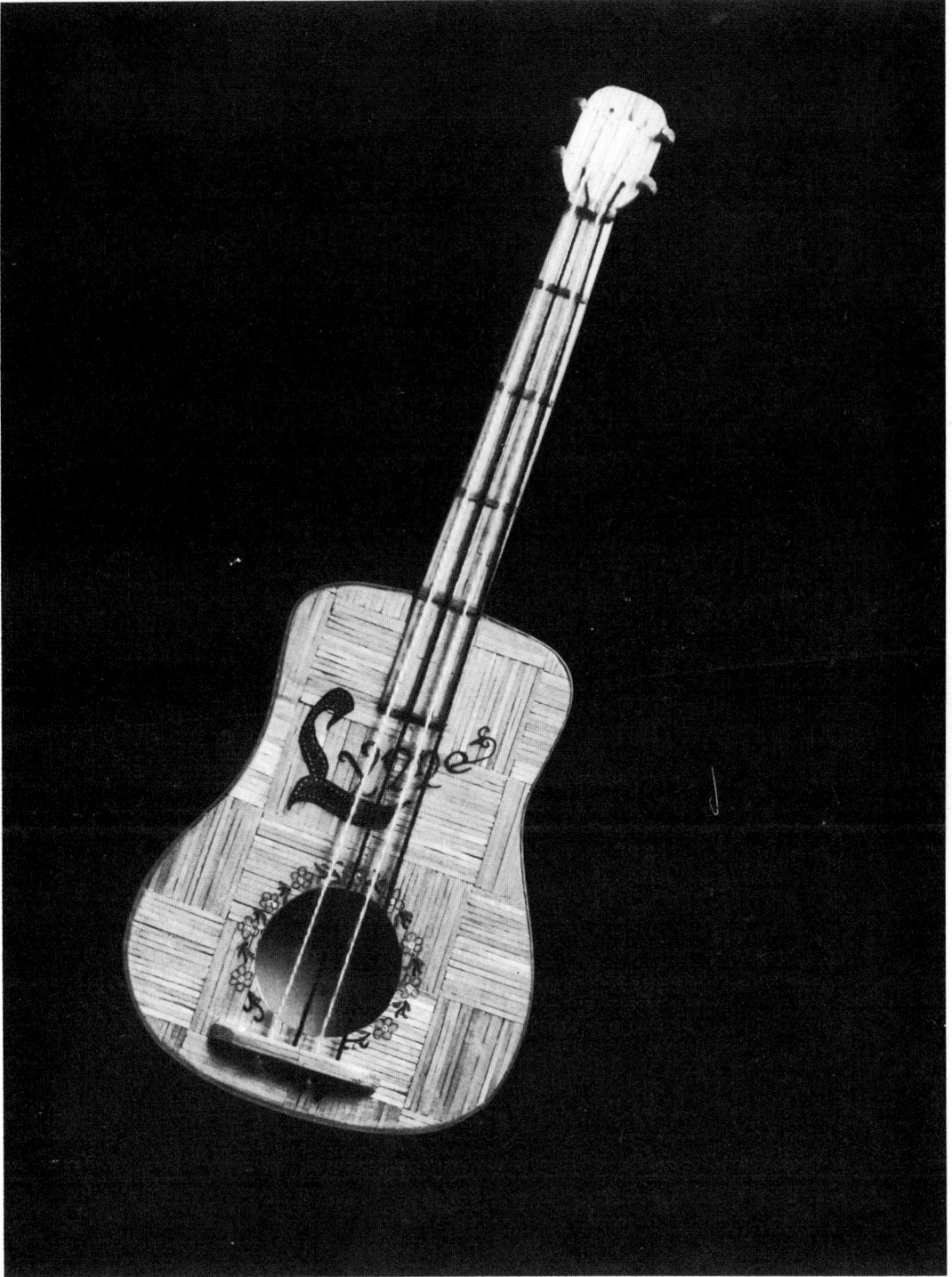

Plate 7: Guitar

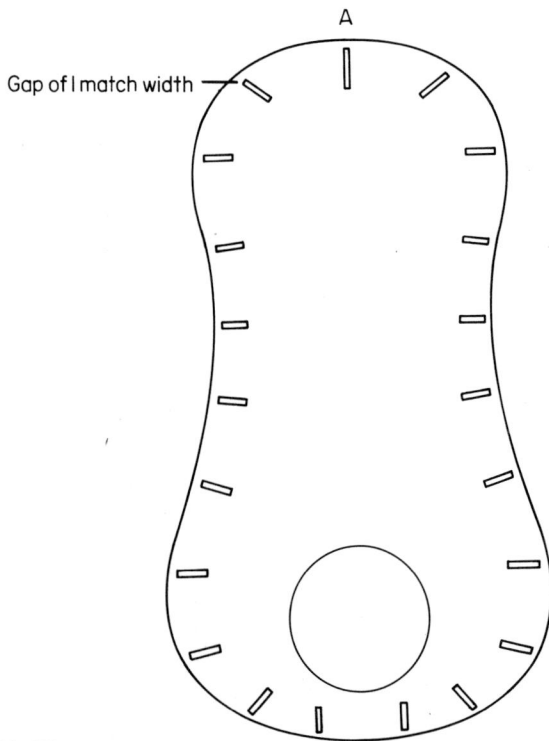

A

Gap of I match width

Fig. 32

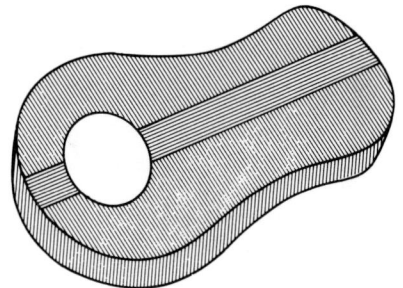

Fig. 33

up against the single matches. When this side is used up, continue with the other. Make sure that they are placed with the matched side on the inside. Trim off if the sides are too long.

Now glue the top or front on top of the sides, making sure that there is a nice tight fit all the way round. Place a weight on top while this is drying.

Then match widthways along the outside of the sides, so that the matches butt up against the outsides of the front and back (see Fig. 33). Allow these to dry for 2–3 hours. Trim off surplus overhang, making sure that the edges are neat. Then sand down to the same smoothness as the rest of the model.

same method, starting at the centre, but lengthways over the whole template. When both sides are dry, place in the press until they are needed again.

Templates 3 and 4 (sides) have to bend, so match them widthways on both sides. Match only one side now and *do not* put in the press, as if the sides are left out they will tend to curl of their own accord and this is a great advantage.

Templates 5 and 6 will form the stem or handle of the guitar. Match template 5 one side at a time, widthways on the face side, lengthways on the reverse. But template 6 must be matched lengthways on *both* sides, in order to curve correctly. Match only one side of template 6 now. Leave template 5 in the press until needed.

Make sure all templates are trimmed and sanded down.

Glue single matches to the reverse sides of the front and back as shown in Fig. 32. Starting at A on the back, glue one of the sides (template 3 or 4) to the edge so that it butts

Handle

Measure back 2.5cm (1in) on the under side of template 5 and apply glue to this area. Glue to the centre top of the main body of the guitar as shown in Fig. 34. Allow at least an hour to dry.

Apply glue along the underneath edges of template 5 and fit template 6 in a curve, matches on the inside, as shown in Fig. 35. Use both hands to hold this in position until the glue begins to set. Push about 8 pins through from the underneath of the edge of template 5 – this will hold the handle in position until dry. Then remove pins and match the outside of template 6. Allow to dry and sand down.

For the end, make up a 2.5cm (1in) square, 2 matches thick. Cut to shape and glue on.

To hold the strings, make 3 solid strips, 2 matches deep, in the following sizes:

1 6cm ($2\frac{1}{2}$in) × 2.5cm (1in)
1 4cm ($1\frac{1}{2}$in) × 15mm ($\frac{5}{8}$in)
1 6cm ($2\frac{1}{2}$in) × 5cm (2in)

Remember to interlock matches when making

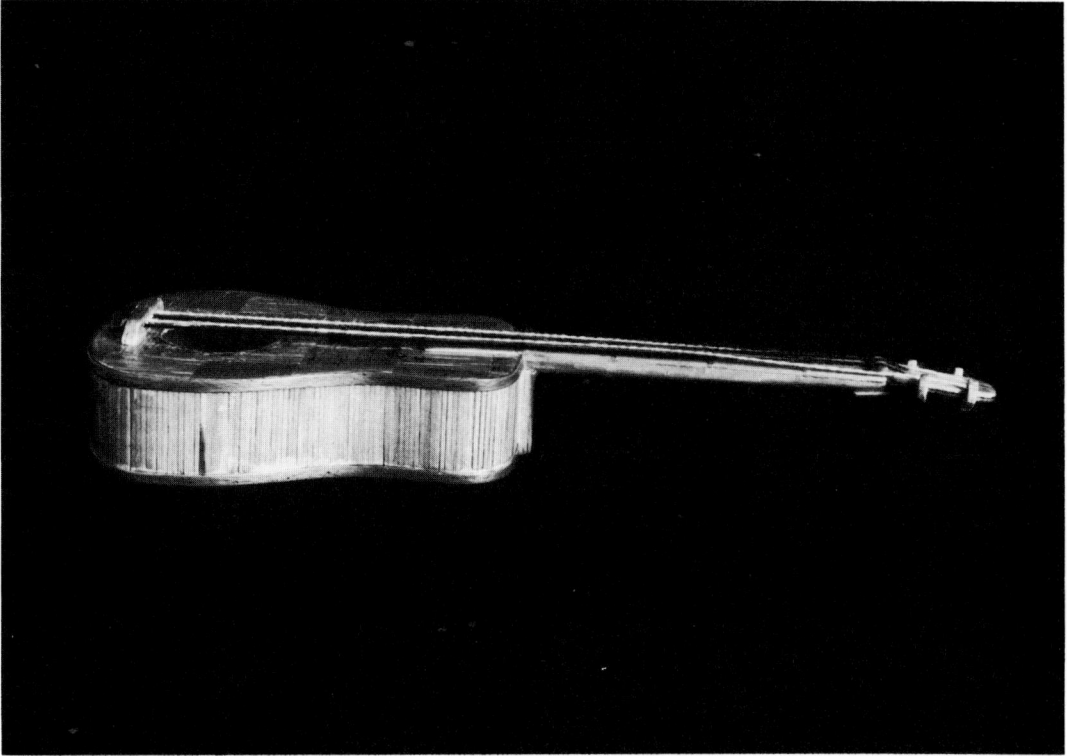

Plate 8: Guitar – side view

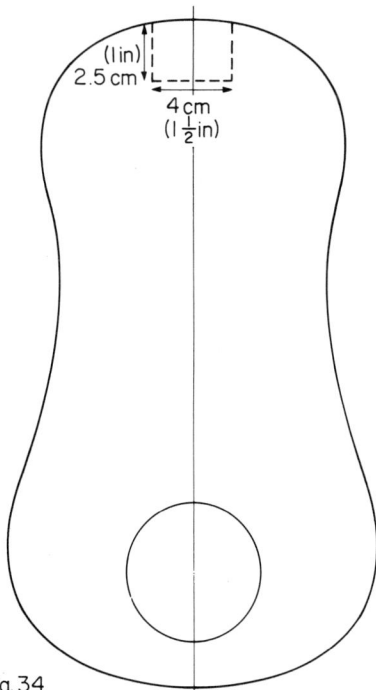

Fig. 34

these. Shape these strips as shown in Fig. 36, and stick pins into part 3. Fit to the main body of the guitar as Fig. 37 (overleaf).

Sand down model all over to a smooth finish removing all surplus glue and indentations. Then apply 3 coats of varnish, rubbing down between each coat and allowing 24 hours to dry between coats.

While the model is drying, cut 5 lengths of string approx. 2.5cm (1in) longer than the length of the guitar. Use paint or dyes to colour these as you wish. Allow to dry. Tie string to pins on the handle, pass through holes in centre

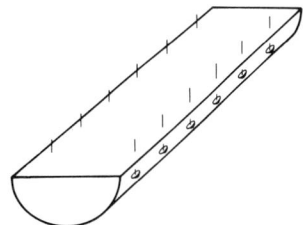

Fig. 35

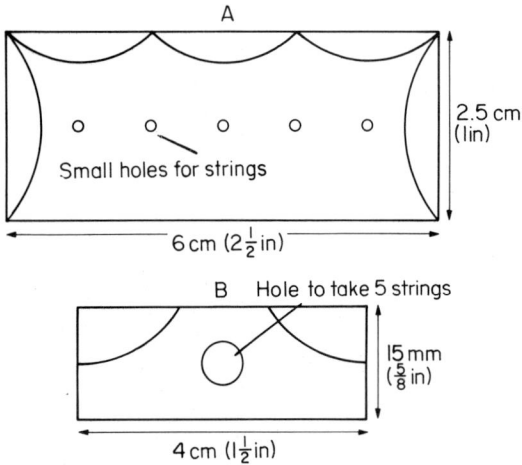

A

Small holes for strings

2.5 cm (1 in)

6 cm (2½ in)

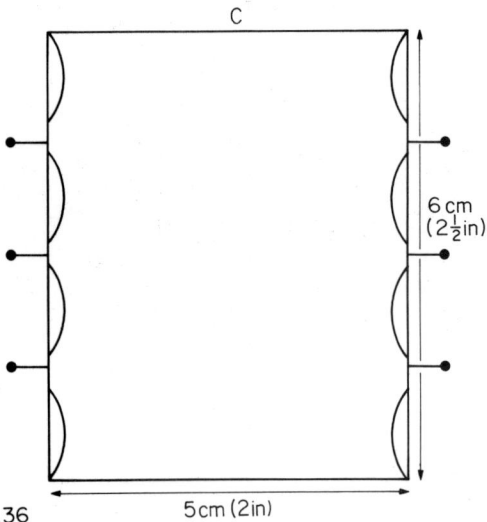

B   Hole to take 5 strings

15 mm (⅝ in)

4 cm (1½ in)

C

6 cm (2½ in)

Fig. 36

5 cm (2 in)

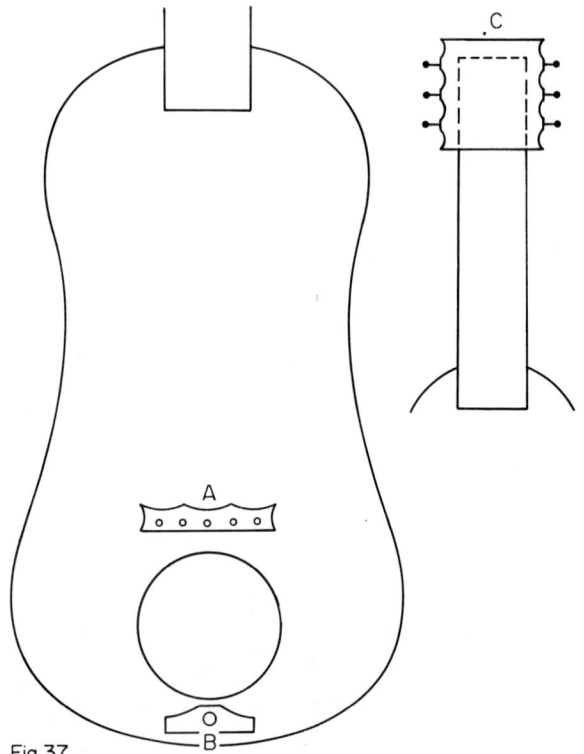

C

A

B

Fig. 37

piece and secure by passing all 5 strings through the hole in the bottom piece, and knotting them.

To finish off the model, add carved matches (p. 11) to cover any template edges showing.

GRANDFATHER CLOCK

The measurements given in this chapter will make a clock that is suitable for a table decoration. However there is no reason why the measurements should not be increased to give a clock of whatever size you like, right up to the height of a real grandmother clock.

You will need:

1500 matches
Cardboard – 225 grams:

3 sheets approximately 35cm (14in) × 26cm (10in)

1 sheet approximately 50cm (20in) × 43cm (17in)

1 sheet thick perspex at least 23cm (9in) × 5cm (2in)

Clock mechanism – from model shop or W. Hobby (see p. 9)

Thin chain and pendulum (optional) available as above

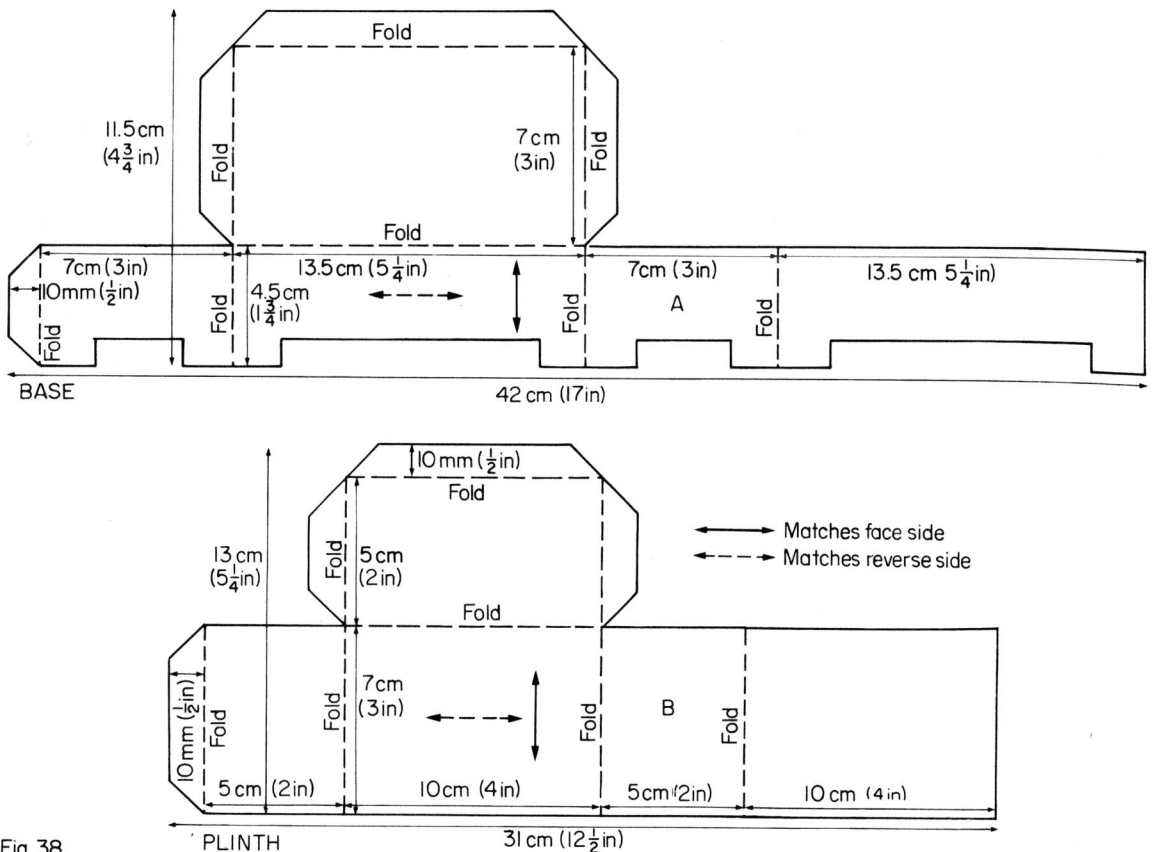

Fig. 38

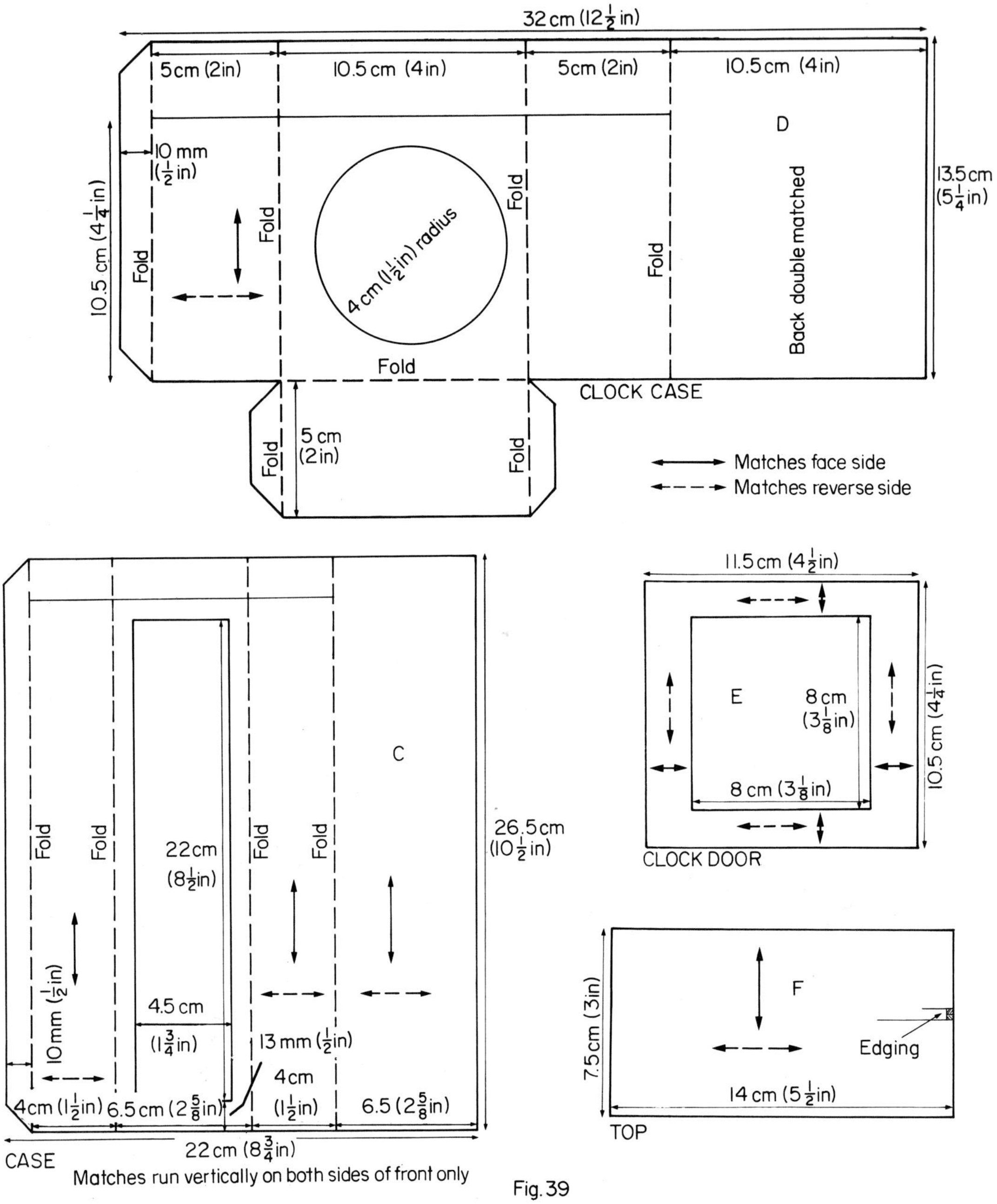

Fig. 39

Draw onto cardboard and cut out templates A–F (Figs. 38 and 39). Mark in folds.

Cut out circle in D and door in C; place door on one side.

Match as shown in 6mm ($\frac{1}{4}$in) stages, one side at a time (Method 1), making sure that matches interlock and remembering to pull each match towards the one already laid, so that the glue sticks them to each other as well as to the template. Leave a gap (1 match width) between sections, to allow for folds. Do not match over joining tabs and on no account fold until the model is ready for assembly.

Trim and allow first sides to dry in the press (p. 10) and then match reverse sides. The matches should run in the opposite direction on all templates except for the front section of C, as shown. Trim and allow to dry in the press, and leave there until they are needed again.

While the templates are drying, make up the other parts in blocks of solid matches.

For G make up 3 blocks 7 matches wide, 7 matches deep; one block 14cm ($5\frac{1}{2}$in) long, the other two 8cm ($3\frac{1}{4}$in) long.

For H, make up 2 blocks 2 matches wide, 2 deep and 11cm ($4\frac{1}{4}$in) long.

For J, make up 2 blocks 2 matches wide, 5 deep and 13cm ($5\frac{1}{4}$in) long; 4 blocks 2 matches wide, 5 deep and 7cm ($2\frac{3}{4}$in) long.

For K, make up 3 blocks 12 matches wide, 8 deep; make one block 13cm ($5\frac{1}{4}$in) long and the other two 7.5cm (3in) long.

Cut and sand these into shape as shown in Figs. 40 and 41. It is useful to lay these out in alphabetical order, otherwise it is easy to confuse some of the smaller parts which look similar.

Rub down all parts well, first with coarse sandpaper then with fine, removing all surplus glue and leaving no indentations.

Fig. 40

Fig. 41

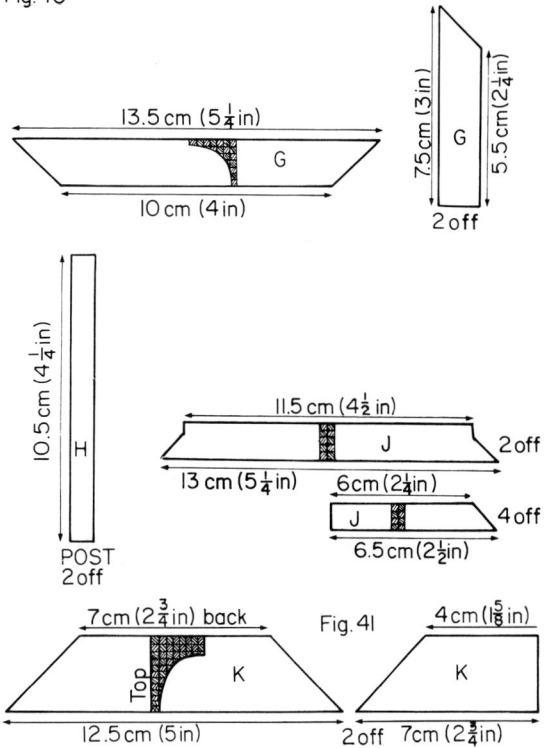

Plate 9: Grandfather clock – detail of plinth

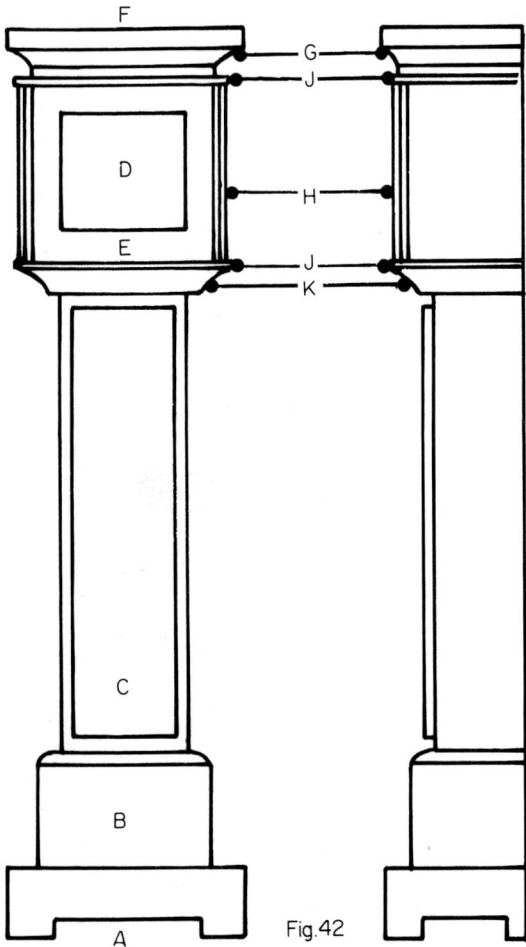

Fig.42

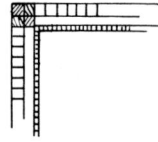

Fig.43

Fig.44

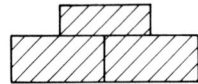

Fig.45

Fig.46

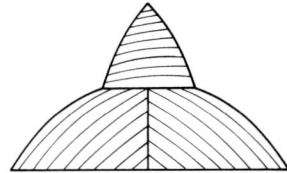

Assembly

First fold and glue together individually parts
A–F as shown, making sure that glueing tabs
fit inside the model.

To assemble, start at the bottom and follow
Fig. 42.

Glue B to the top of A, then C to the top of
B. Leave just enough time between these stages
for the glue to get tacky.

Glue K to the top of C, first the sides, then
the front, and D on top of K.

Glue G (sides first, then front) on top of D
and finally F on top of G.

Now glue E flat against D.

Glue the side pieces of J to the sides of D and
then the front pieces of J along the top and
bottom of E.

Glue side pieces H along the sides of E,
between Js.

Corner joints

To fill in the corners, make up blocks 4 matches
square, the required length, allow to dry, sand
and glue into place (Fig. 43).

Finish off along the top of B with blocks of
matches 5 wide, 2 deep, and sand to a curve
as in Fig. 44.

Cover any templates still showing either with
strips 2 matches wide, laid along the edge, or
with carved matches (p. 11).

Carving

An alternative way of carving matches, as
opposed to that mentioned above, is shown in
Figs. 45–6.

Make a dozen or so strips 2 matches wide,
approx. 25cm (10in) long, with matches
interlocking. Allow to dry. Then lay a line of
single matches, interlocking, in the middle of
each strip as shown. Allow to dry. Lightly
sandpaper the single match into a pointed
shape as in Fig. 46.

Plate 10: Grandfather clock

Plate 11: Grandfather clock – detail of simple painted face

Cut strips to the lengths you require. Fix some fine sandpaper round a round pencil. Use this alternately with a fine modelling knife to shape the pointed match as shown.

Door
Place door template onto the sheet of perspex, draw around the edge with a pencil and cut out. For the frame, glue a single line of matches round both sides. Sand down lightly. Then hinge with headless pins and add handle as for the church doors (p. 23).

When the model is complete, sand down with a worn piece of fine sandpaper so that all parts are perfectly smooth, then apply three coats of varnish. Rub down lightly between each coat and allow 24 hours between coats to dry.

The clock workings simply sit inside the circular hole in D.

GRAND PIANO

This model can be made up either as a straight-forward model, or as a jewellery box, lined with velvet, or as a musical jewellery box with the addition of musical works.

You will need:

3000 matches
Cardboard (225 grams) for templates:
   1 20cm (8in) × 22cm (8½in) lid
   1 20cm (8in) × 24cm (9½in) base
   2 46cm (18in) × 4cm (1½in) sides
   1 20cm (8in) × 4cm (1½in) keyboard back
   1 20cm (8in) × 3cm (1¼in) keyboard lid
Musical works – available from model shops, in particular W. Hobby (see p. 9).

Cut out templates.

Mark lid and base as shown in Fig. 47, remembering that the base is 2.5cm (1in) longer. Use compasses to get the curved line then cut round the shape of the piano.

The pattern shown in Fig. 48 is useful to follow as cuts have to be made in this part and laying the matches as shown leaves a clean straight edge to work with.

Match in stages from the straight front edge, trimming matches to the curve. When complete place in the press to dry. When dry, match reverse sides, trim and replace in the press until needed.

Match the back of the keyboard on both sides

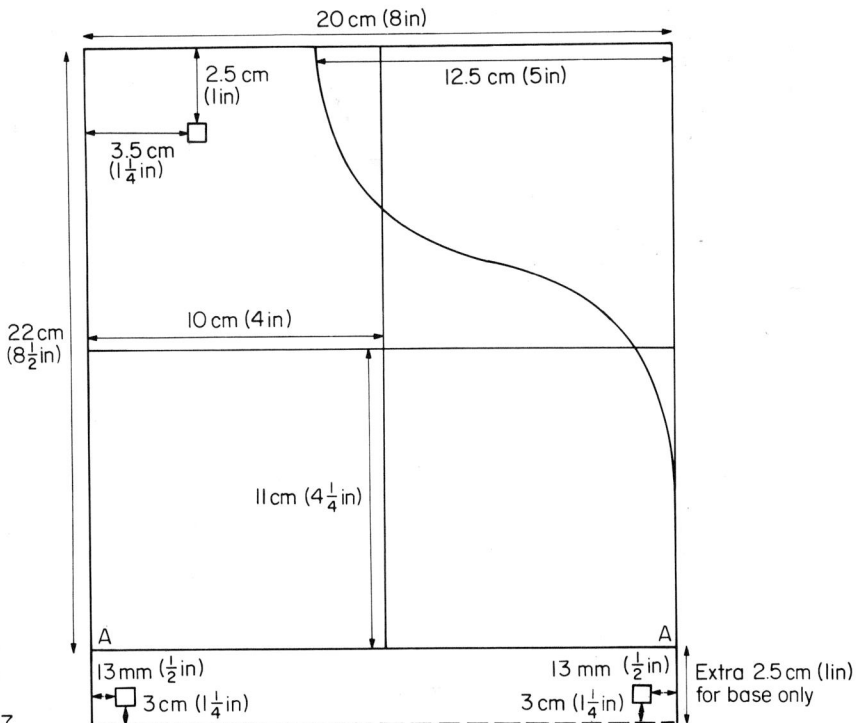

Fig. 47

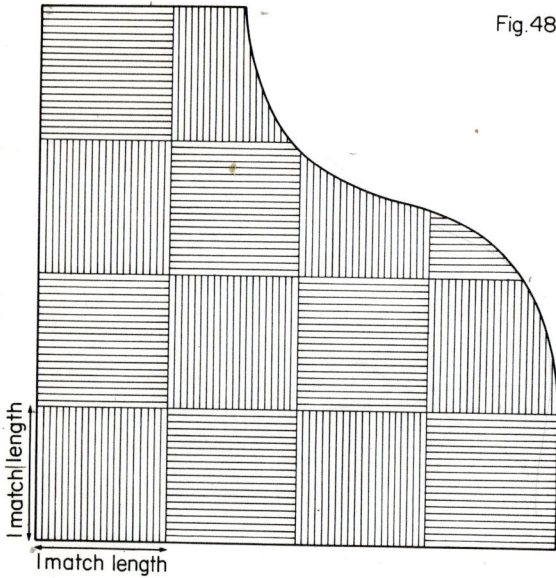

Fig. 48

1 match length

1 match length

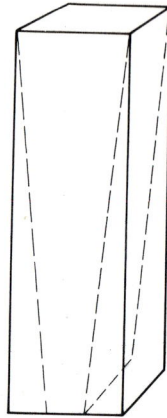

Fig. 49

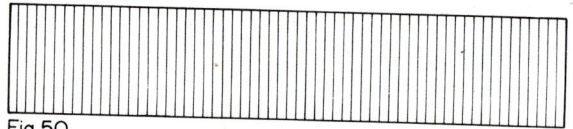

Fig. 50

as Method 1, with the matches running horizontally on the face side, vertically on the reverse. Remember to interlock matches. Place in press until needed.

While these are drying, make up legs. Make up 4 blocks 3 matches long, 3 matches wide, 3 matches deep. Allow to dry and sand to a smooth finish, tapering them at one end as shown in Fig. 49.

When the lid, base and back are dry, sandpaper to a smooth finish, first with a coarse sandpaper and then with fine. Make sure that all surplus glue is removed from the surface and that there are no indentations.

Match sides as shown in Fig. 50 (on both sides, one at a time) with the matches going the same way on the reverse because the sides must be flexible in order to bend round the frame of the piano. Do not place in the press but put to one side to dry.

Assembly

On the base, glue a row of matches between the front and the line 2.5cm (1in) back, see Fig. 51.

Glue lightly along the bottom of the keyboard back and fix it to the base along the line, up against the line of matches (see Fig. 51). Place a weight on the row of matches and

against the back to hold it upright in the correct position. Allow to dry thoroughly before assembling any more parts.

On the lid, draw a line 2.5cm (1in) back from the front edge, then cut along it with a sharp knife.

Hinge lid as shown in Fig. 52. Place the two sections of the lid, A and B, on a flat surface.

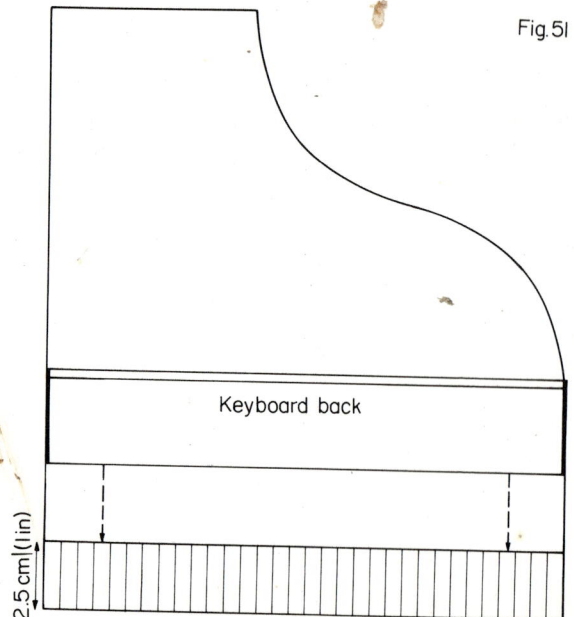

Fig. 51

Keyboard back

2.5 cm (1in)

42

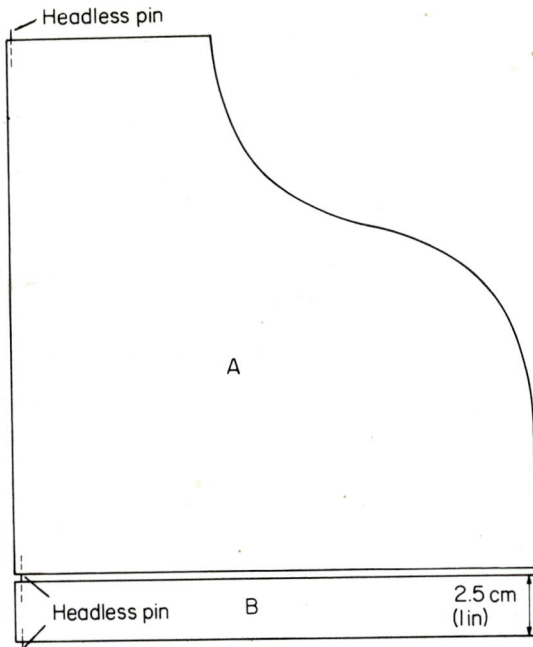

Fig. 52

Headless pin

A

Headless pin   B   2.5 cm (1 in)

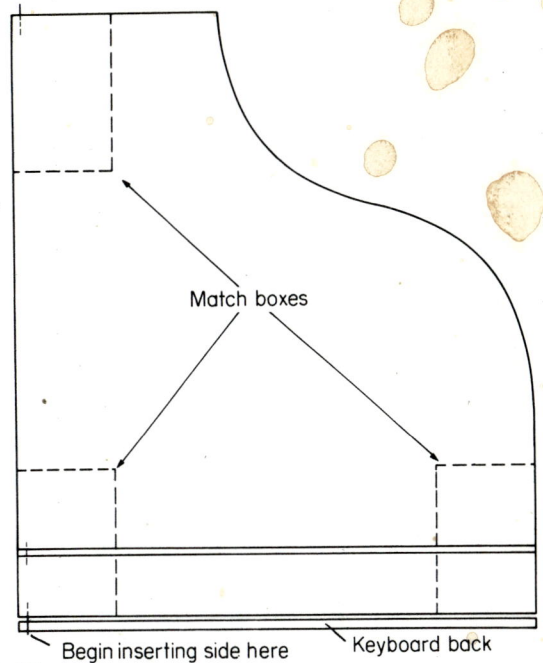

Fig. 53

Match boxes

Begin inserting side here   Keyboard back

Remove the heads from two dressmakers' pins. Insert one pin at each end of A, and then use the pin at the front to join A and B. Insert the pin at the front of the lid (B) into the back of the keyboard, so that the lid lies flush with the top of the back. Place matchboxes between the base and the lid for support as shown in Fig. 53.

Smooth down the edges of the two side pieces. Then glue lightly along the bottom edge of one piece and insert between the lid and the base, starting at the keyboard end as shown and inserting the pin at the other end of A into the side as you go round. Take care not to dislodge the keyboard back while doing this.

When this piece is used up, continue with the other side piece until you have gone completely round the piano to the other side of the keyboard. Cut off any surplus and put to one side.

Lay the model upside-down on a flat surface and apply a weight which covers the whole of the model and distributes pressure evenly. Allow to dry and remove all surplus glue with sandpaper.

Lift the hinged part of the lid out of the way and glue a single line of matches round the inside of the sides as shown in Fig. 54 to support the lid so that it lies flush with the top of the sides.

To finish off the keyboard, cut single matches to half the width of the keyboard; these can be either dyed or painted black and placed in position as the black keys.

Keyboard sides
Take 2 pieces of the surplus sides and trim so that they are the width of the keyboard and approximately half the height of the keyboard back. Glue these firmly to the edges of the keyboard and the keyboard back, as can be seen in plate 12 on p. 44.

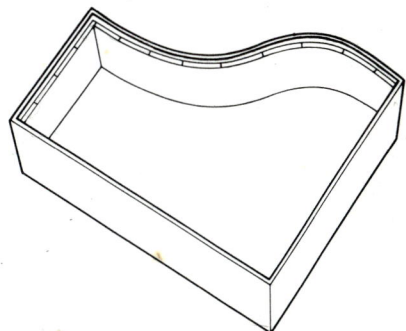

Fig. 54

Keyboard lid

Match template lengthways on both sides, one side at a time, remembering to interlock matches as Method 1. *Do not* put in the press to dry. If left out, it will begin to curve of its own accord. Trim and sand to a smooth finish.

Place in position between keyboard sides and mark the curve on the sides. Then trim or sand the sides to this curve.

Use pins to hinge the lid to the keyboard sides. Drive a headless pin into each of the keyboard sides, so that the pins go into the keyboard lid. Drive pins in well and cover with a tiny piece of match to hide them. Sand down well.

When the lid is fitted, lay a row of carved matches (p. 11) right along the back of the keyboard, immediately above the top of the lid and the keyboard sides.

To hold the main lid up at the correct angle, make a prop 2 matches wide, 2 matches deep and 10cm (4in) long. Allow to dry and sand with a fine sandpaper. Stick one ½-match to the lid near the keyboard end of the piano. The prop will fit inside the base of the piano, on the ridge of matches which supports the lid when closed, and butt up against the ½-match ridge in the lid.

Glue legs into position as shown in Fig. 47.

Before varnishing, check that all traces of glue and all indentations are removed.

Apply 3 coats of varnish, rubbing down lightly between coats and allowing each 24 hours to dry.

If you wish to make the piano into a musical box or jewel box, follow the instructions for fitting musical works and lining with velvet on pp. 28–9.

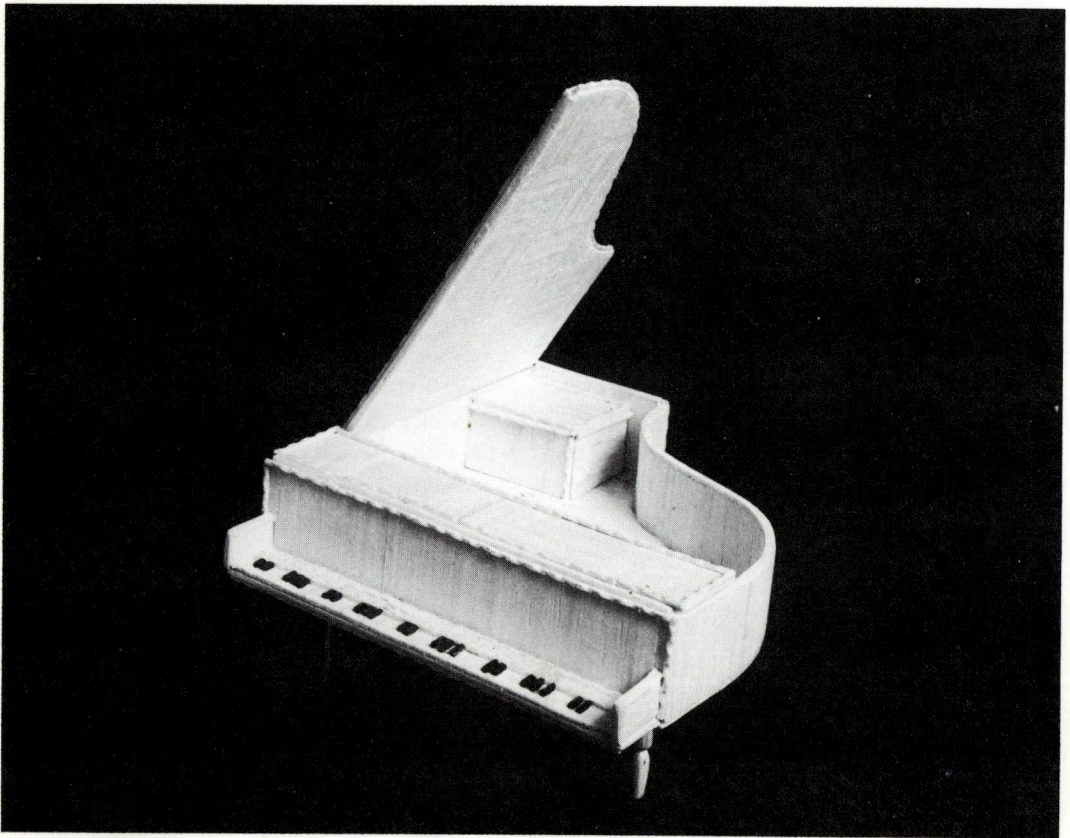

Plate 12: Grand piano

WINDMILL

You will need:

3500 matches

Cardboard – 225 grams for templates:
  1 20cm (8in) × 20cm (8in) base
  1 10cm (4in) × 10cm (4in) base for upper housing

Cardboard – 160 grams for templates:
  4 15cm (6in) × 27cm (10½in) front, rear and sides

2 8cm (3¼in) × 5cm (2in) sides for upper housing
2 8cm (3¼in) × 7.5cm (3in) front and rear, upper housing
1 8cm (3¼in) × 5cm (2in) roof

Perspex – thin, 1 sheet 7.5cm (3in) square

First cut out template of base; then 4 sides as in Figs. 55 and 56. Make sure that you cut out templates very accurately, or the model will not

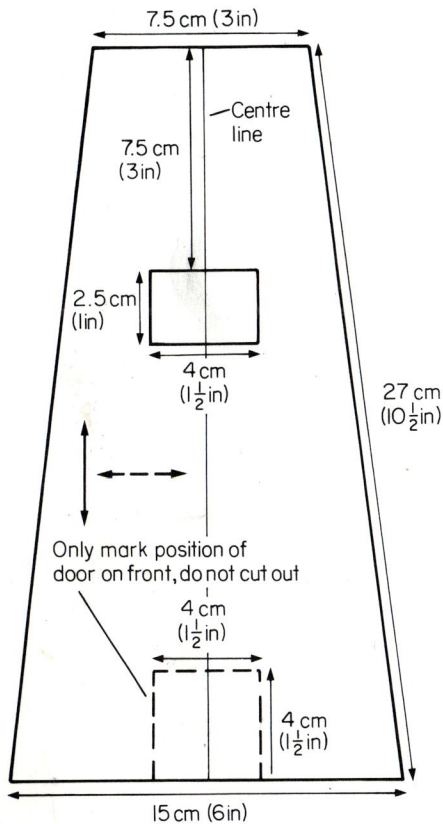

7.5 cm (3in)

Centre line

7.5 cm (3in)

2.5 cm (1in)

4 cm (1½in)

27 cm (10½in)

Only mark position of door on front, do not cut out

4 cm (1½in)

4 cm (1½in)

15 cm (6in)

Front and rear

→ Matches face side
--→ Matches reverse side

Fig.55

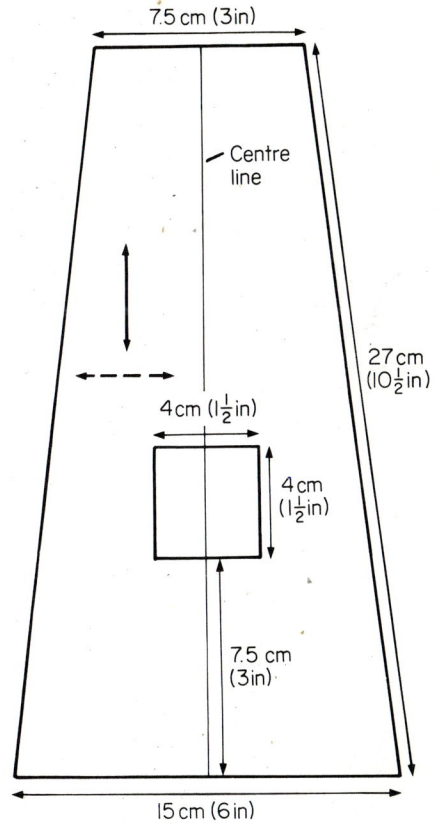

7.5 cm (3in)

Centre line

4cm (1½in)

4cm (1½in)

27 cm (10½in)

7.5 cm (3in)

15 cm (6in)

Sides

→ Matches face side
--→ Matches reverse side

Fig.56

assemble correctly. Cut out windows as marked and put on one side.

With this model it is better to match all components on one side first and place them in the press until ready for matching on the other side.

Match base as Method 1, on one side only at first, remembering to interlock matches and to pull them together so that they stick to each other as well as to the template. Match sides vertically on the face side, beginning at the centre line and working outwards.

Make sure that the window openings are well trimmed at this stage; otherwise when you fit the perspex panes it will be obvious that they are out of alignment with the whole.

Place base and sides in the press and allow to dry for 2 hours.

Before matching the reverse of the sides, fit the windows. Cut out windows in perspex, making them 6mm ($\frac{1}{4}$in) larger all round than the window templates already cut out.

Glue round the edge of the perspex and press into position around the window openings. Allow to dry.

Then match the four sides on the reverse, making sure that the matches run in the opposite direction to those on the face. Place in the press and allow to dry.

When the four sides are dry, mark out the unmatched side of the base as in Fig. 57. Then glue a line of matches along the outside of line A to form a rim.

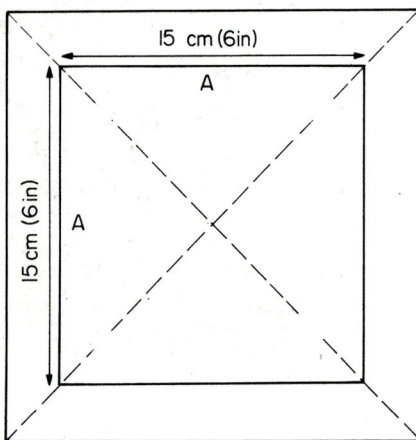

Fig.58

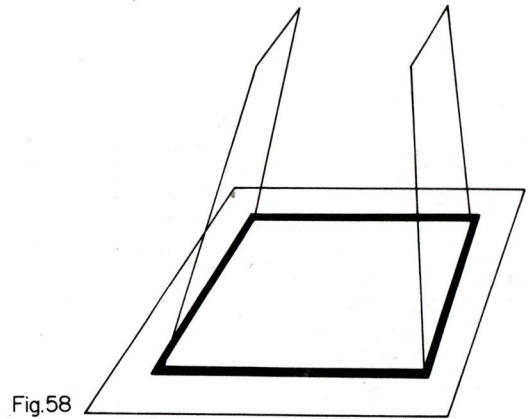

Check that the 4 sides will stand inside this rim, then glue generously round the inside of the rim and position 2 opposite sides as in Fig. 58. Ask a friend to hold these in position and then put a thin line of glue along the bottom inside edge of the front and back, fit into position with the glued side against the rim, and secure with 2 elastic bands, as shown in Fig. 59.

To ensure that the model stays in the right position while drying, cut out a square of cardboard 7.5cm (3in) square and fit into the opening at the top as in Fig. 59. This can either be left in position as a strengthening factor for the body or removed once the glue has dried.

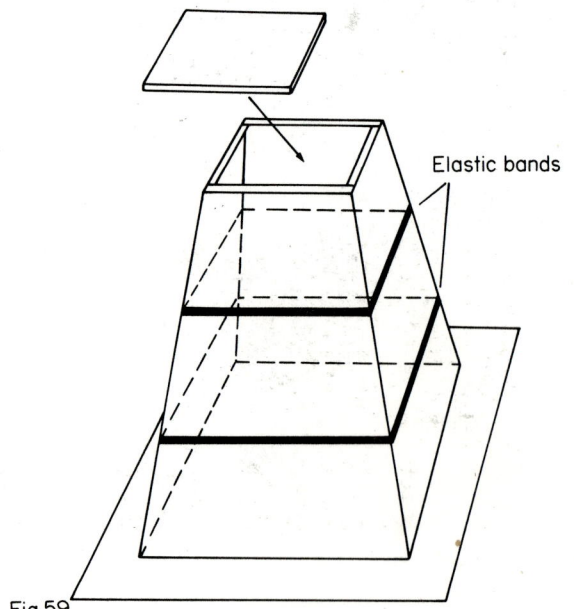

15 cm (6in)

A

15 cm (6in)

A

Fig.57

Elastic bands

Fig.59

Plate 13: Windmill

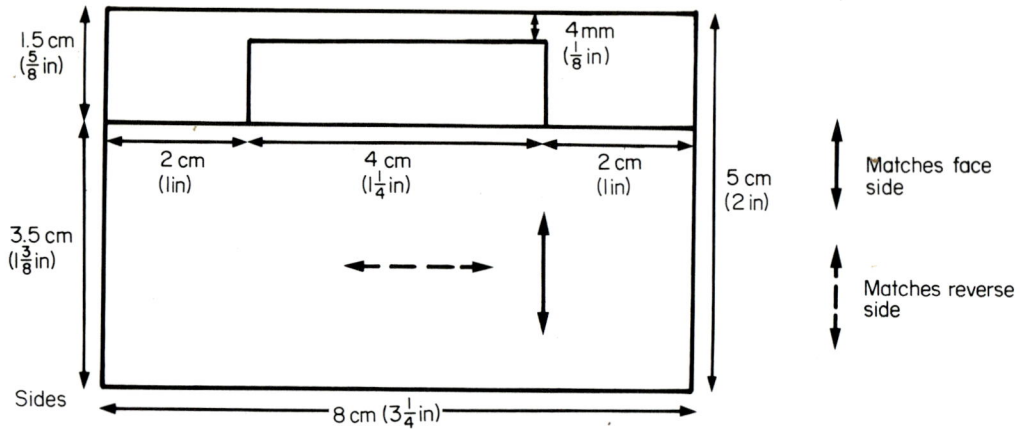

Fig.60   Sides

1.5 cm ($\frac{5}{8}$ in)

4mm ($\frac{1}{8}$ in)

2 cm (1in)

4 cm (1$\frac{1}{4}$ in)

2 cm (1in)

5 cm (2 in)

3.5 cm (1$\frac{3}{8}$ in)

8 cm (3$\frac{1}{4}$ in)

Matches face side

Matches reverse side

If it is to be removed, make the piece slightly smaller so that it comes out easily.

If you do not have a friend there to help you, fit a square of cardboard into the bottom of the windmill as well, to hold the sides in position as you put on the elastic bands. Allow to dry.

Upper housing

Cut out templates for 4 sides, roof and base, as above measurements. Mark sides and back and front as shown in Figs. 60 and 61. Cut out windows; and roof shape of front and back.

Match the sides on the face side only at first, as shown. Place in the press and allow to dry.

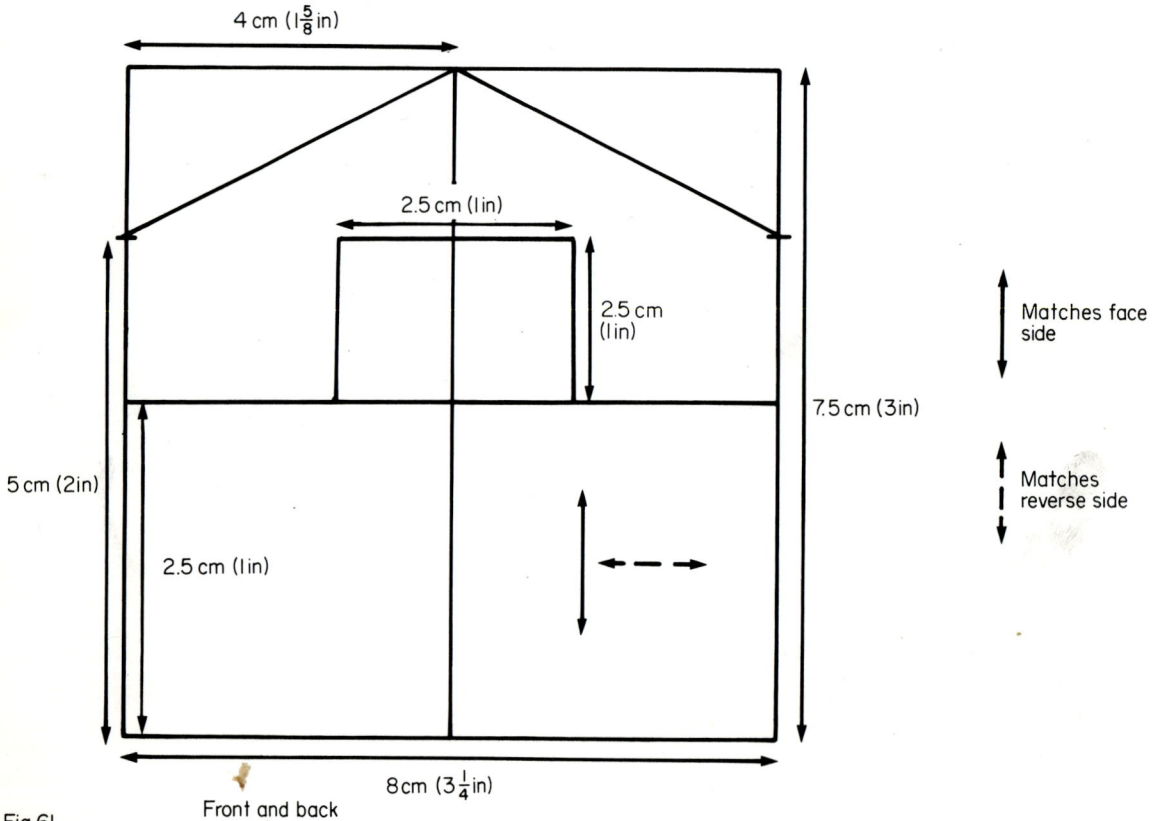

4 cm (1$\frac{5}{8}$ in)

2.5 cm (1in)

2.5 cm (1in)

7.5 cm (3in)

5 cm (2in)

2.5 cm (1in)

8cm (3$\frac{1}{4}$ in)

Matches face side

Matches reverse side

Front and back

Fig.61

48

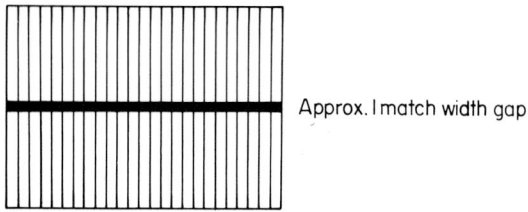

Fig.62

Approx. 1 match width gap

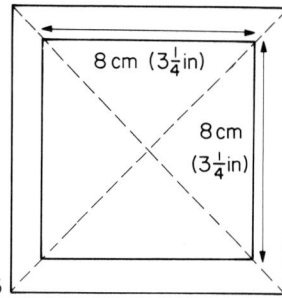

Fig.63

8 cm (3¼in)

8 cm (3¼in)

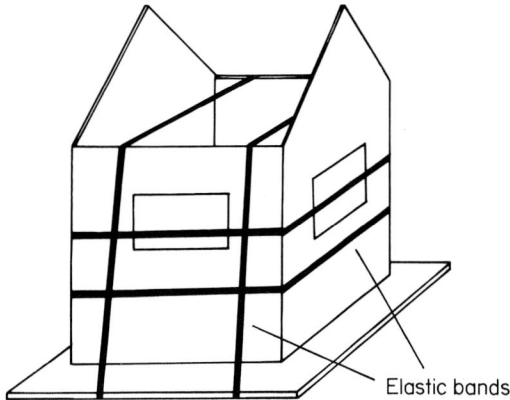

Fig.64

Elastic bands

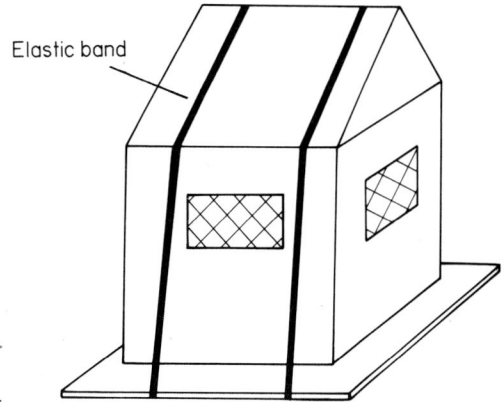

Elastic band

Fig.65

Then insert perspex windows as for the main body of the windmill.

Match the base on both sides, remembering to match in opposite directions on either side.

Match the roof as shown in Fig. 62, leaving a space for the fold and running the matches in the same direction on both sides. Place all parts in the press to dry until needed again.

Assembly

Mark the base as shown in Fig. 63 and make a rim as for main base. With help from a friend, position the four sides and secure with elastic bands as shown in Fig. 64. Allow to dry.

To fit the roof, glue along the top of the 4 sides and fix the roof firmly on top of them. Secure with elastic bands (Fig. 65). Allow to dry.

In the same way, glue round the top of the main windmill and fix the base of the upper housing firmly to it, securing with elastic bands. Allow to dry.

Sails

For the crossmembers, glue 2 matches together and repeat this process at least 50 times.

Then make up 12 long stretchers, 3 matches wide, 1 match deep, 30cm (12in) long. To ensure that these run in a straight line, lay the first row along the edge of a ruler.

While these are drying, sand down the small crossmembers.

When they are dry, sandpaper the long strips to a smooth finish, but do not put too much pressure on them as they snap quite easily.

With a sharp knife, square off the ends of the long strips.

Cut 8 of them to a length of 20cm (8in) and 4 to a length of 24cm (9½in).

To make one sail, place one long stretcher between 2 shorter ones. Glue crossmembers across the long strips as shown in Fig. 66, at intervals of roughly 2cm (¾in). Do this right along to the end of the 20cm (8in) strips, leaving the centre one to overrun by 4cm (1½in). Then make 3 more sails in the same way.

When all 4 sails are complete and dry, lay out

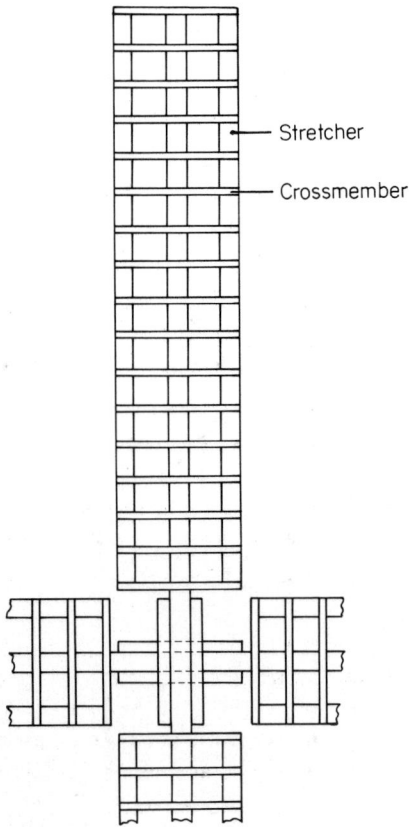

Stretcher

Crossmember

Fig.66

Fig 67

Fig.68

flat, overlap long centre sections as shown in
Fig. 66, and glue together in the middle. Lay
sails flat to dry.

Wind vane
Make up 2 strips 2 matches wide, 9cm (3½in)
long. Allow to dry, then fix single matches
across them at either end as shown in Fig. 67.
Lay one across the other and glue together.

For the vane supports, make up two strips 2
matches wide, 2 matches deep and 15cm (6in)
long, remembering to interlock one layer on top
of the other to add stability.

While the supports are drying, make up
another block 3 matches wide, 3 matches deep.
Allow to dry and sandpaper to a smooth finish.

Before the sails and wind vane can be
attached, the main body of the windmill must
be finished.

Complete the matching of the base of the
main windmill by glueing matches on to the
upper side and pressing them tightly against the

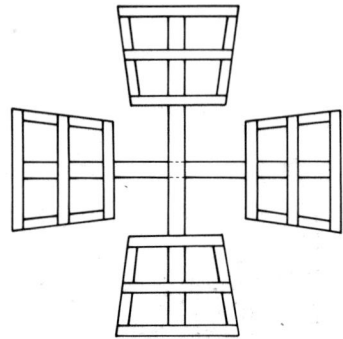

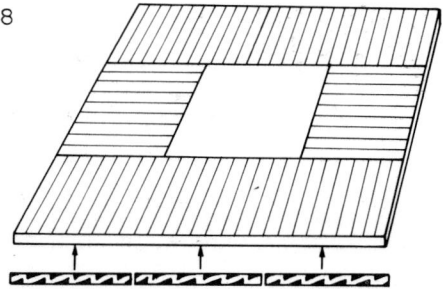

housing, allowing the overlap to be at the
outside of the base (Fig. 68). Allow to dry and
trim with a knife to obtain a clean edge.
Lightly sandpaper and glue carved matches
(p. 11) round the edge to conceal the template.

Corner joints
Make up 4 strips 2 matches wide and 4 strips
3 matches wide, both 27cm (10½in) long, for
the main windmill corners. For the upper
housing make up 4 strips 2 matches wide, 4
strips 3 matches wide, both 5cm (2in) long.
Allow to dry and sand.

Attach the wider strip to the side of the
windmill, allowing 1 match width to overlap
the corner. Then stick the narrow strip to the
adjoining side so that it butts up against the
overlapping match to make a neat finish (see
p. 23).

Supports
The supports are all 1 match long. Glue into
position as shown in Fig. 69, 2 on each side and
1 at each corner.

Decorating the model
To decorate the plain surfaces of the windmill,
glue strips 2 matches wide, 1 match deep, well

Plate 14: Windmill – detail of upper housing

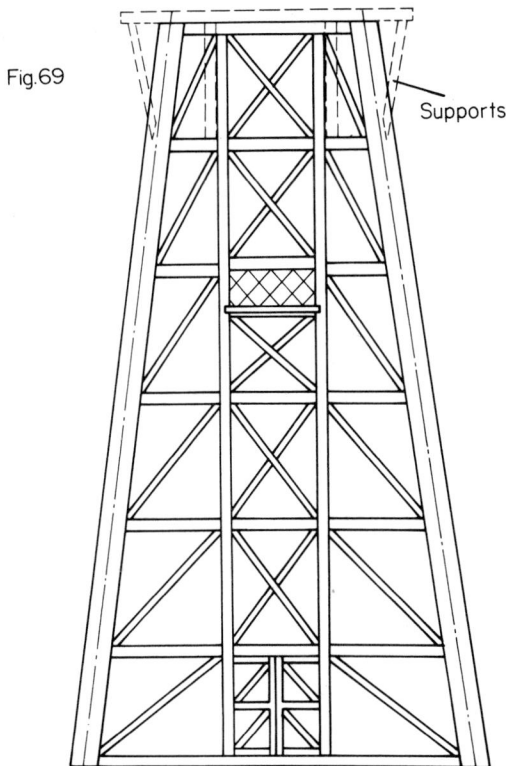
Fig. 70

sanded down, down the corners of the model as in Figs. 69 and 70, which show further possible decorations using these strips.

Stick single rows of carved matches (p. 11)

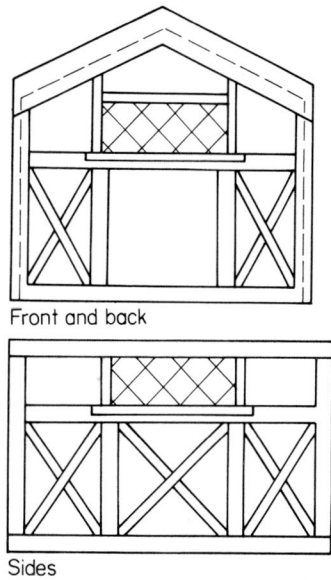
Fig. 69

Supports

onto any part where the template shows through: round the edges of the upper base, windows, along the top of the roof etc.

The false doors are formed simply by sticking on 2-match wide strips as in Fig. 69.

Fixing the sails and wind vane
Take the block of matches 3 wide and 3 deep already made up, measure two-thirds along the block and cut through. Fix the larger portion to a central point in the front of the upper housing, above the window, and the smaller portion to the sails as shown in Fig. 71.

Allow to dry, then push a large dressmakers' pin all the way through both sections and into the housing as shown.

To fix the wind vane: use a ruler to find the

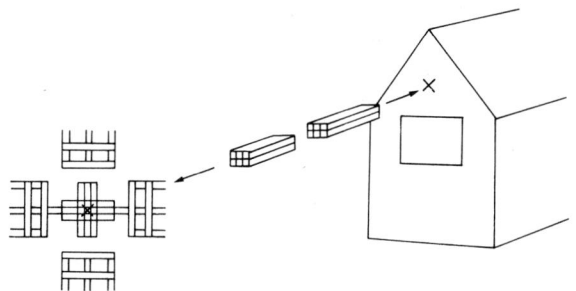
Fig. 71

51

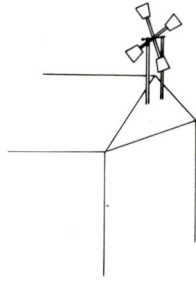

Fig.72

Then push a dressmakers' pin through the 2 strips and through the centre of the wind vane as in Fig. 72 and cut off any surplus pin that protrudes.

When the windmill is complete, make sure that it is well sanded down and that no glue is visible. Then apply 3 or 4 coats of varnish, rubbing down lightly between coats and allowing 24 hours for each to dry.

centre of the back of the housing. Glue the 2 vane supports on either side of the centre, positioning so that they extend approximately 6cm (2½in) above the point of the roof. Leave enough room between them for the wind vane to hang freely.

Fencing

If you wish to complete the model by putting fencing round the windmill, construct as described on p. 23 and glue round the edges of the base.

Plate 15: Windmill – detail of decoration and fencing

BARREL-TOP CARAVAN

You will need:

10,000 matches
Perspex – thick, 1 sheet 10cm (4in) × 22.5cm (7in)
6mm ($\frac{1}{4}$in) drill
Fretsaw
Tracing paper
Greaseproof paper
Small nail
Thimble
Fine chain or cotton
Small weight
Cardboard – 225 grams for templates:
  1 29cm (11$\frac{1}{4}$in) × 14.5cm (5$\frac{3}{4}$in) base
  2 23.5cm (9$\frac{1}{4}$in) × 4cm (1$\frac{1}{2}$in) sides
  2 21cm (8$\frac{1}{4}$in) × 21cm (8$\frac{1}{4}$in) front and back

Cardboard – 160 grams for template:
  1 39cm (15$\frac{1}{4}$in) × 23cm (9in) roof

Using a compass, mark front and back as in Figs. 73 and 74 and cut out caravan shape. Cut out doors and windows and put on one side.

Base
Match the base so that the matches run in different directions on either side of the template. They should run *widthways* on the face side, *lengthways* on the reverse. Match one side at a time, in 6mm ($\frac{1}{4}$in) stages (Method 1), remembering to interlock the matches (Fig. 2).

When the first side is complete, place in the press and allow to dry for 2 hours. Then trim with a fine modelling knife.

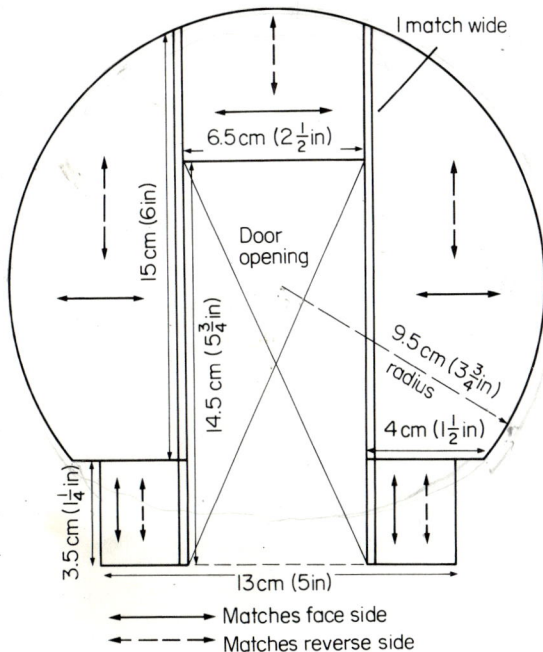

Fig.73   Front

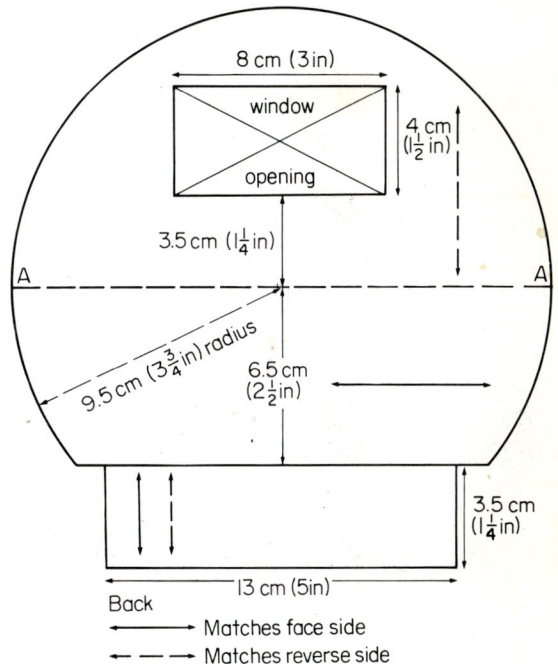

Fig.74

53

Match the reverse side and replace in the press until required.

Sides

Match the sides so that the matches run *lengthways* on the face side, *widthways* on the reverse. Match in exactly the same way as the base, making sure that the edges are trimmed very straight as they play an important part in putting the model together.

Front and back

The front and back should be matched on both sides, as shown in Figs. 73 and 74. Start at the bottom edges and work up, using the same method as for the base.

Match the face sides only at first. Place in the press and allow to dry. Then trim edges and sand until smooth.

For the window on the back use a sheet of perspex. Place window template on perspex, draw round the edge with a pencil, then draw another frame, 6mm ($\frac{1}{4}$in) larger, round this and cut out. If you wish, use a needle to mark the window as shown in the door windows in Fig. 76.

To fit the window, put a small amount of glue round the window opening on the reverse side of the back and place the perspex over the opening. Put a small weight on top to hold in position while drying.

When this is dry, match the reverse sides of the front and back as shown in Figs. 73 and 74. Trim the edges and place in the press until needed again.

When the back is dry, add the window frame to the face side. Just glue a single line of carved matches (p. 11) round the window opening.

To make the back into the correct shape, draw line A (Fig. 74) on the back and measure the width of the back here. Then cut along line A. Make up a strip 5 matches wide, 2 deep and the length of line A. Remember to interlock matches. Allow to dry and sand down. Then join top and bottom of back with this strip as Fig. 75.

Door

Place the door template onto a sheet of

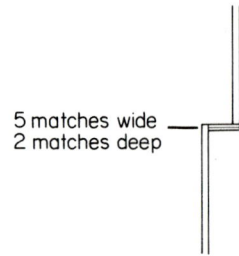

5 matches wide
2 matches deep

Fig.75

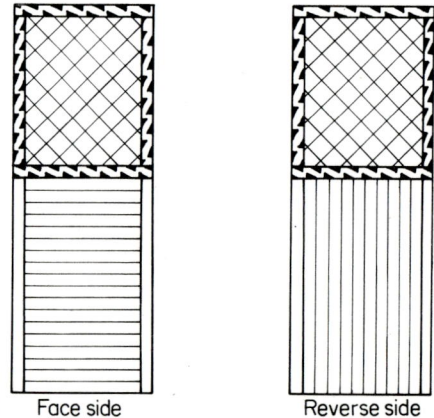

Fig.76   Face side   Reverse side

perspex and draw round it in pencil. Cut out and divide equally in half. Match the lower parts on both sides, as Fig. 76. There is no need to keep these in the press while drying as the perspex will stop them from warping. Allow to dry.

Then glue a frame of single matches (carved if you like (p. 11)) round the perspex of the upper part of the door. Use a needle to make diamond-shaped panes.

Assembly

Make sure that all the components matched so far are properly trimmed with pincers or a modelling knife, all surplus glue removed and rubbed down, first with coarse sandpaper and then with fine.

Joining the front, back and sides to the base: from the front edge of the base measure back 4cm ($1\frac{1}{2}$in) on either side and draw a faint pencil line there across the upper side of the base.

Make sure that the two side pieces are both the right length (23.5cm – $9\frac{1}{4}$in) and use one of these to measure from your pencil line to the rear of the base. Mark the place with a dot. Do

Plate 16: Barrel-top caravan

this at both sides and then draw a pencil line across to join the dots. This gives the correct measurement for the body of the caravan.

Glue lightly along the bottom of the front and then fix to base on the inside of the front pencil line, making sure that it is the right way round (ie face side outwards) and perfectly upright. To keep it in position, put a wedge or a weighted tin next to it.

Glue the back to the base on the inside of the other pencil line in the same way, again making sure that the face side is outwards. Allow at least 24 hours for these to dry. Then try the sides in position, with the front and the back fitting between them. Glue into position and allow to dry until the glue is hard enough to hold them.

Roof
Cut out the roof template and pin this lengthways against one side of the bodywork, allowing a 5cm (2in) overlap at either end of the base (Fig. 77).

When it is pinned into position, roll the cardboard tightly over the top of the caravan as shown and pin. Then mark where the bottom edge of the roof will come on either side (ie at the top of the sides) and draw a pencil line across the cardboard at this point. Remove the template from the model and make sure the lines are perfectly straight. Cut along the pencil lines.

The roof must be matched with the matches running lengthways on both sides, or the roof will not be able to bend. Remember to interlock the matches. Match on the reverse side only at first, in 6mm ($\frac{1}{4}$in) stages. When it is complete, allow to dry for 2 hours but *do not* put in the press. Just put to one side for about 24 hours after it is dry and during this time it will begin to bend to the shape of the roof by itself.

Fixing the roof
When the roof is dry, trim off any surplus of matches at either end. Glue into position over the back and front, with the matches on the *inside* of the curve. Use elastic bands to hold tightly, leaving no gaps between the body and the roof. Allow at least 24 hours to dry before

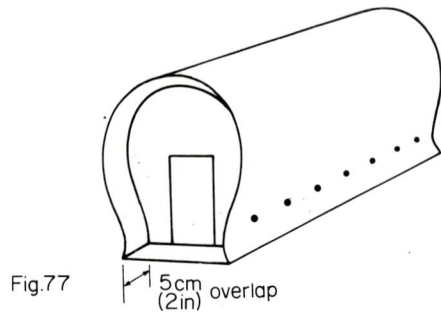

Fig.77   5cm (2in) overlap

attempting to remove the elastic bands.

Before matching the outside of the roof, mark the shape of the roof ends on the template as shown in fig. 77. Do this with a light pencil mark and cut through carefully with a fine fret saw so that you do not break away any matches or leave a rough edge to the underside of the roof.

When you match the outside of the roof, try to avoid using any matches that are kinked or bent – these gaps will show when the roof is completed and rubbed down. They cannot even be hidden using a filler, as when varnished the filler will be clearly visible.

The basic shell of the caravan is now complete and the rest of the model is made entirely of matches. No more templates are needed.

Hay rack
Before making this, add stretchers to the back of the caravan. Glue 4 part-matches, 2cm ($\frac{3}{4}$in) long, to the underneath of the overhang on the back, so that they protrude slightly. Carve (p. 11) and sand down 4 matches and glue to these protruding ends and to the lower part of the back (see plate 17 opposite).

For the hayrack, draw over Fig. 78 on a piece of tracing paper. Place this onto your working board and match over the design, glueing the matches directly onto the tracing paper. Remember to interlock the matches. Build this up into 2 layers of matches, 2 wide. Allow time to dry.

Remove the tracing paper and sand down to a smooth finish, sanding off any remains of tracing paper. Carve the edges of the rack as shown.

Plate 17: Caravan – detail of back

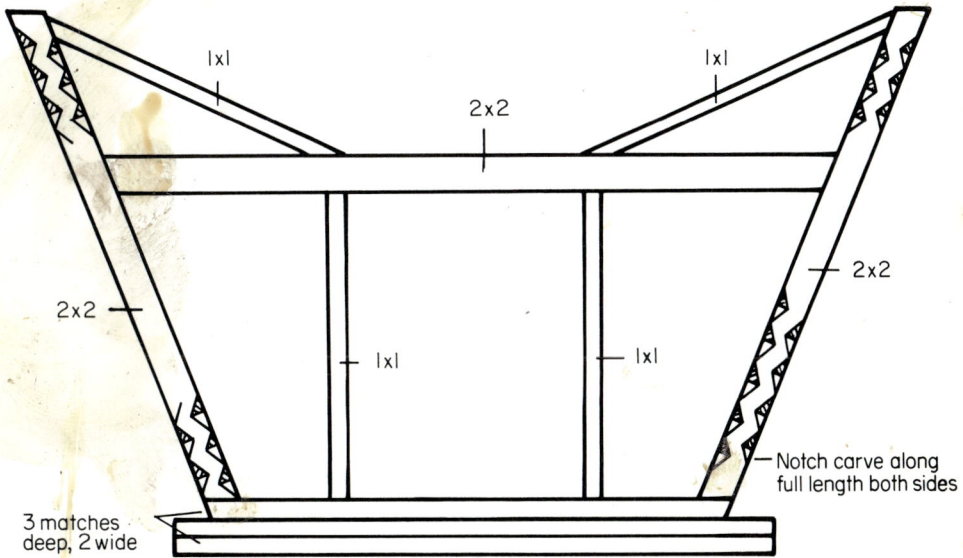

|x|

|x|

2x2

2x2

2x2

|x|

|x|

Notch carve along
full length both sides

3 matches
deep, 2 wide

Fig. 78

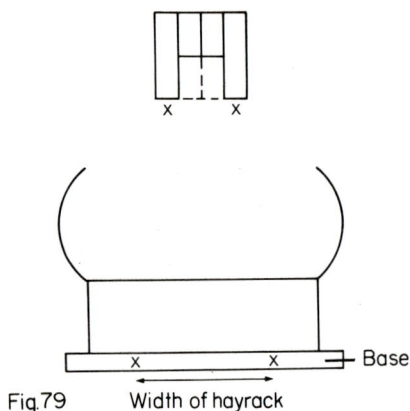

Fig. 79 Width of hayrack

Hubs: place a layer of greaseproof paper round the shaft of a round pencil. Glue one layer of matches all the way round the shaft on top of the greaseproof paper. Allow a few minutes to dry, then slip the paper from the pencil. Repeat 4 times. This will give you enough for 4 hubs and hub caps.

Assembly: place another piece of tracing paper on the working board and trace round the shape of the wheel in Fig. 80. Drive a small nail into the board through the centre of the tracing. Cut about 13mm ($\frac{1}{2}$in) off one of the hubs and glue centrally over the top of the nail.

Then glue the spokes into position as marked, remembering to glue one end to the hub. Allow to dry for 24 hours and remove tracing paper.

Sand off all surplus glue and replace over the tracing paper and nail. Cut the blocks which form the rim to fit between each set of spokes. Glue into position, allowing 24 hours for drying.

Repeat this process for the other small wheel, and, using Fig. 81, for the 2 big wheels. When dry, sand down to a smooth finish.

To fix the hay rack to the caravan: make up 2 blocks, 4 matches wide, $\frac{1}{2}$ match long. Allow to dry and sand down. Then cut out $\frac{1}{2}$ of the 2 centre matches as shown in Fig. 79. Glue sides x of one of the hooks to the base of the caravan as shown.

Insert base of hay rack into both hooks and glue the second hook to the caravan as the first.

Attach the top of the hay rack to the stretchers with cotton or with a fine chain.

Wheels

For the wheels, make up 100 blocks 3 matches wide, 2 matches deep, 1 match long to form the outside rims; 100 blocks 2 matches wide, 2 matches deep, 1 match long for the spokes. Carve as shown on Figs. 80 and 81.

Front and rear axles

Make up two strips 4 matches wide, 4 deep and 5cm (2in) longer than the width of the caravan. Allow to dry and sand down, removing all surplus glue.

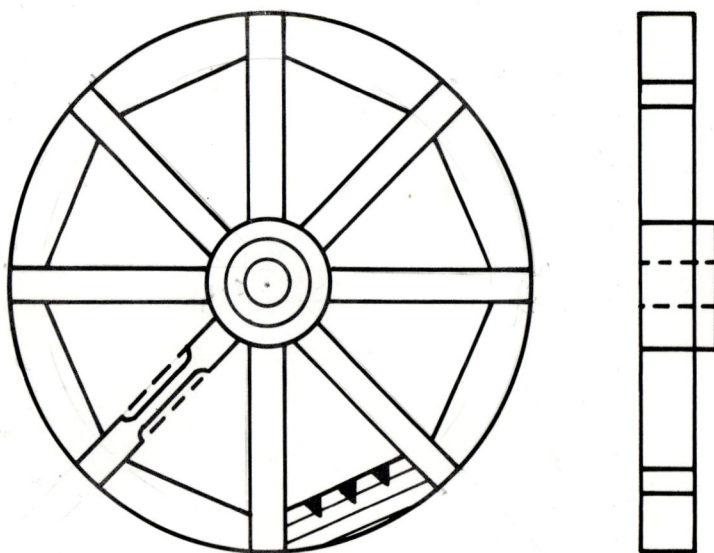

Fig. 80

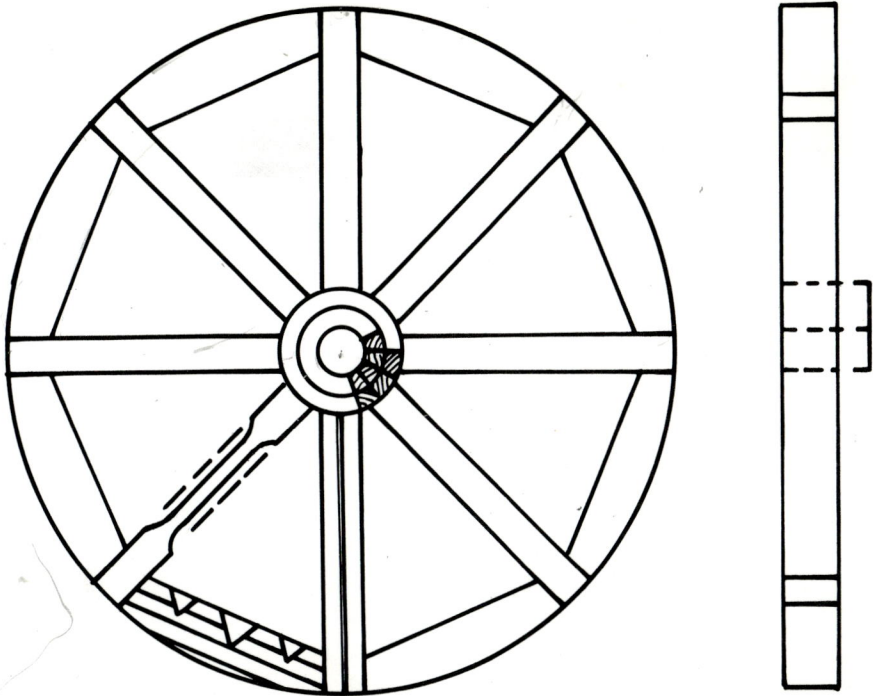

Fig. 81

The front wheels must be fitted so that they come under the base and in a line with the side of the caravan above (see plate 19). So cut one axle down so that it protrudes only 13mm ($\frac{1}{2}$in) beyond either side of the base.

Use a sharp knife to trim off ends of front axle until you have a round peg which fits snugly into the hub of the front wheels and protrudes slightly beyond it as Fig. 82. To keep the wheels in place, fit the remainder of the hub over the protruding axle on the outside of the wheel, to form the hub cap.

The rear wheels are fitted so that they stand outside the base, with the top rim just slightly higher than the base, (see plate 17). Therefore trim the rear axle less, so that it still protrudes enough to carry the hub and wheel beyond the base; fit rear wheels to axle as front wheels.

Springs
The front and back springs are made up of strips of matches 3 wide and 1 deep, cut to size as Fig. 83 and with a part match laid between each leaf.

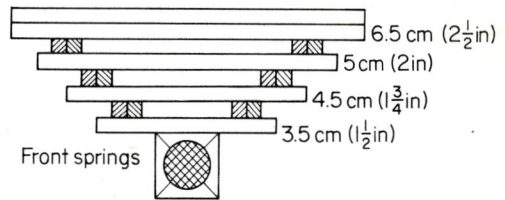

6.5 cm (2$\frac{1}{2}$in)
5cm (2in)
4.5 cm (1$\frac{3}{4}$in)
3.5 cm (1$\frac{1}{2}$in)
Front springs

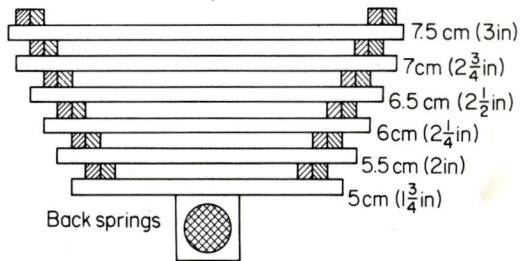

7.5 cm (3in)
7cm (2$\frac{3}{4}$in)
6.5 cm (2$\frac{1}{2}$in)
6cm (2$\frac{1}{4}$in)
5.5 cm (2in)
5cm (1$\frac{3}{4}$in)
Back springs

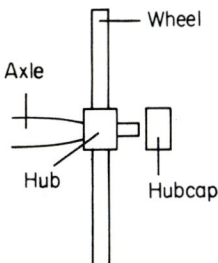

Wheel
Axle
Hub
Hubcap

Fig. 82

Fig. 83

Plate 18: Caravan – detail of underneath of base

The front springs have five leaves, the back six. Make up strips and leave to dry. Then glue leaves together, with part matches in between, as shown.

Runners

For runners make up 2 strips 3 matches wide, 2 deep and 29cm (11$\frac{1}{4}$in) long; 3 strips 3 matches wide, 2 deep and 14.5cm (5$\frac{3}{4}$in) long.

Glue shorter strips across base as shown in Fig. 84. Allow to dry. Then glue 2 long strips as shown, making joints at places marked *b*. Allow to dry.

Glue back springs to base and, when this is dry, rear axle to springs.

Turntable

Make up 2 strips 4 matches wide, 4 deep, 11cm (4$\frac{1}{2}$in) long, and 3 strips 4 matches wide, 3 deep, 8cm (3$\frac{1}{8}$in) long. Remember to interlock the matches. Glue together (Fig. 85 over) and allow to dry. Use 11 single matches to form a platform

between B and C. When this is dry, glue a layer of matches going in the opposite direction on the underneath. Then glue single matches between A and B as shown. Trim and sand down when dry.

Drill a 6mm ($\frac{1}{4}$in)-diameter hole in the middle of the platform.

Glue front springs to outside edges of turntable as shown. Allow to dry, then glue front axle to springs.

Shafts

Make up 2 strips 5 matches wide, 4 matches deep, 21cm (8$\frac{1}{4}$in) long and 2 strips 4 matches

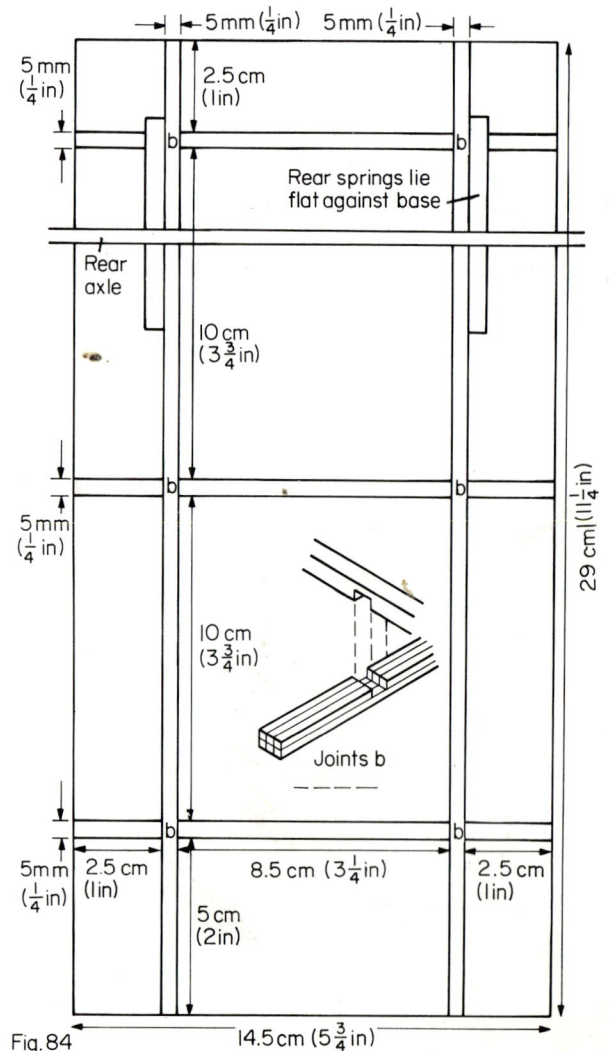

Fig. 84

5mm ($\frac{1}{4}$in)   5mm ($\frac{1}{4}$in)

5mm ($\frac{1}{4}$in)

2.5cm (1in)

Rear springs lie flat against base

Rear axle

10cm (3$\frac{3}{4}$in)

5mm ($\frac{1}{4}$in)

10cm (3$\frac{3}{4}$in)

Joints b

5mm ($\frac{1}{4}$in)   2.5cm (1in)   8.5cm (3$\frac{1}{4}$in)   2.5cm (1in)

5cm (2in)

14.5cm (5$\frac{3}{4}$in)

29cm (11$\frac{1}{4}$in)

Plate 19: Caravan – front view showing decoration and barrels

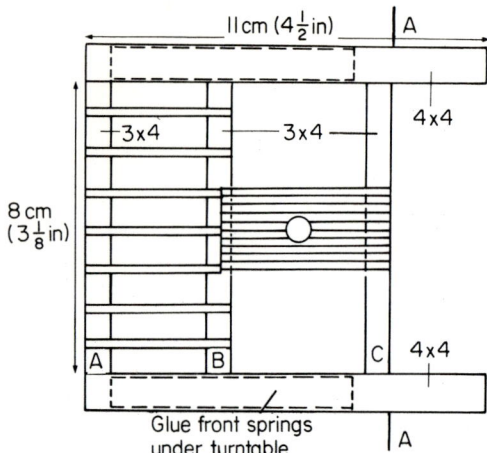

11 cm (4½ in)

A

3x4 — 3x4

4x4

8 cm (3⅛ in)

4x4

A   B   C   4x4

Glue front springs under turntable

A

Fig.85   Pin parts in place while glue is drying

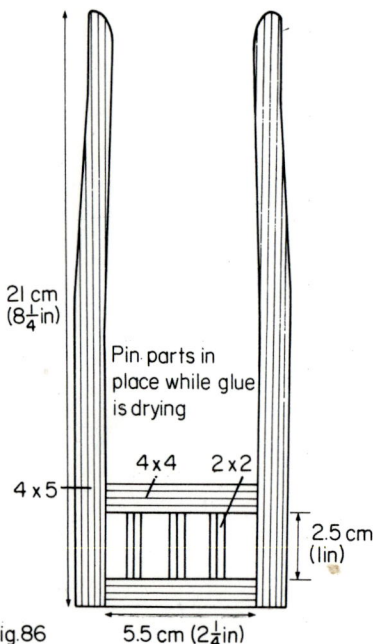

21 cm (8¼ in)

Pin parts in place while glue is drying

4x5   4x4   2x2

2.5 cm (1in)

Fig.86   5.5 cm (2¼ in)

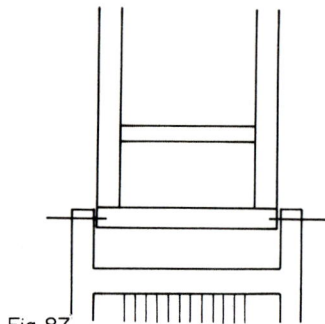

Fig. 87

Make up a peg slightly smaller than the hole, for a loose fitting. Make up a block 2 matches deep, the same size as the platform on the turntable. When dry, bore a 6mm (¼in) hole in the centre.

Glue the peg into this hole. Allow to dry, then glue to the place marked on the bottom of the base.

The hingeing of the door is usually left until the end in case you wish to furnish the inside of the caravan. Simply hinge with headless dressmakers' pins and add handles as for the church doors (p. 23).

Decorations
The decorations and carvings on the model are left entirely to the individual modeller. On the caravan in plate 16 I have used carved matches of 2 different sorts (see pp. 11 and 38) along edges to cover the template wherever it shows, and for extra decorations on the back, sides and front.

The edges of the roof at either end have been painted. If you decide to do this, remember to give them one coat of varnish before painting, to avoid the paint running.

Also shown are buckets and barrels. Make the buckets as for the wishing well (p. 18). Make up the barrels by glueing together 2 buckets and then sanding into shape.

When the model is complete, make sure that all parts are well sanded down and that all traces of glue have disappeared. Then apply 3 coats of varnish, allowing 24 hours between coats to dry and rubbing down lightly between each coat.

wide, 4 deep and 5.5cm (2¼in) long. Remember to interlock matches. Glue together as Fig. 86. Trim and sand down when dry.

Hinge shafts to turntable using dressmakers' pins, as shown in Fig. 87. Trim off any pin that protrudes.

Fitting the turntable to the caravan
Line up the turntable under the caravan so that line A is level with the front of the caravan. Mark the bottom of the base through the hole and round the platform as far as possible.

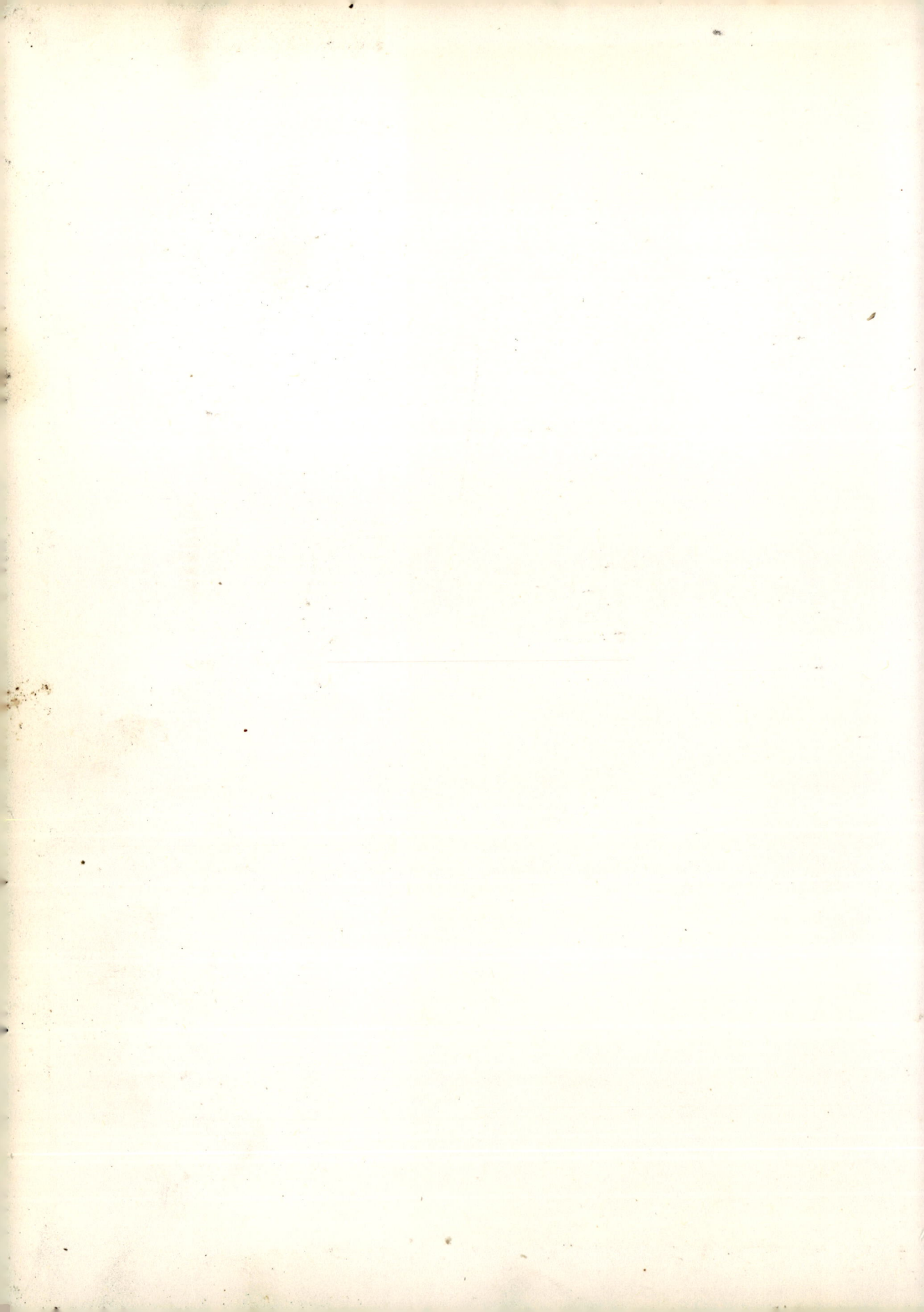